I Love
CHAMPAGNE

I Love CHAMPAGNE

by Davy Żyw

FREIGHT BOOKS

First published 2017

Freight Books
49-53 Virginia Street
Glasgow, G1 1TS
www.freightbooks.co.uk

A CIP catalogue reference for this book is available from the British Library

ISBN 978-1-910449-93-6
eISBN: 978-1-910449-94-3

Typeset by Freight
Printed and bound in Poland

the publisher acknowledges investment from
Creative Scotland toward the publication of this book

Although my Granny preferred sherry,
this book is for her.

Contents

Introduction	1
Champagne and me	2
Man on a mission	4
Origins	7
Early doors	7
The first fizz	8
Méthode traditionnelle	9
King and country	14
The region	17
How the British invented champagne (nearly)	17
Sweet tooth	19
War	20
Success story	21
Toasting to victory	22
The four pillars of taste	26
Sweetness levels	27
Champagne styles	28
Classification	32
Seven factors of flavour	33
Fizz with food	38
Know your glasses	41
Bottle sizes	46
Price index	47

The champagnes	49
André Clouet	51
AR Lenoble	54
Armand de Brignac	58
Billecart-Salmon	60
Bollinger	66
Clos Cazals	71
Charles Heidsieck	76
Delamotte	82
Deutz	87
Didier Chopin	90
Dom Perignon	94
Gosset	102
J.L. Vergnon	104
Jacquesson	108
Krug	112
Lanson	118
Laurent Perrier	122
Le Mesnil	130
Louis Roederer	132
Moët & Chandon	140
G.H. Mumm	144
Perrier-Jouët	148
Pol Roger	150
Pommery	158
Ruinart	162
Salon	166
Jacques Selosse	172
Taittinger	176
Veuve Clicquot	180
Virginie T	186
Glossary	190

Introduction

Champagne is delicious. This is very important. It's scrumptious and magnificent. I love its flavour; I love its fizziness. I love the sense of drama and celebration it brings to any occasion. Champagne's associations with success, partying and enjoyment are as ingrained in the wine as the bubbles themselves. As the godfather of champagne famously said: 'Brothers, I'm drinking stars!' Dom Perignon had obviously had a few glasses at this point, but his quote is poignant nonetheless, drinking champagne is liquid heaven.

I want to share with you my passion for the fizz, and in doing so give insight into how champagne has earned its eternally glamorous status, champagne is the drink with which we celebrate life. It marks our milestones, in a way no other drink can. There is always an excited intake of breath when the bottle pops. Most champagne bottles have close to six atmospheric bars of pressure within them, a similar pressure found in a double-decker bus tyre. This danger and tension in opening a bottle is unique to champagne; it is both sexy and dramatic. We experience excitement and anticipation even before the first sip. It gets the party started. It fuels us with adrenalin and brings theatre to our lives. New Year wouldn't be the same without the pop of a champagne cork and foaming frothy flutes on the tables and in the hands of the swaying drinkers. When we raise a glass to toast, it's fizzing.

But for all the drama and allure, ultimately it's the drink itself which has made champagne such an irresistible and popular choice for millions of drinkers over the past four centuries.

It hasn't been one long party for the men and women of the Champagne region of North East France. Like much of continental Europe wines have been made there since Roman times, but their look and taste have changed over the centuries. The region, and its wines, have had a turbulent history: revolutions, a couple of invasions, economic turmoil, two world wars and a vineyard pest which literally ate 99% of all the vines in the region at the beginning of the 1900s. Times have been tough, like the production of champagne itself, this has been no quick process; it has taken time, sweat, blood, tears and a helluva lotta love. This history makes it all the more marvellous that champagne has survived and thrived.

The 50 champagnes in this book are my favourites and also significant somehow to champagne's success. I have discovered these beauties in the course of my last twelve years in the wine industry, and have painstakingly tasted each and every bottle. We'll go through each of the champagnes and houses to find out why they are important to champagne's story. While this is an ice bucket list of champagnes to try, no list is definitive and I recognize that everyone has their own preferences when it comes to their favourite fizzer. However, I can, hand on heart, say the Champers in these pages will rock your socks off. I promise that it's worth saving those pennies and every so often cashing them in for a bottle or two of the world's greatest drink.

Champagne and me

I have worked within wine for over a decade. I started in a basement wine shop in Edinburgh, and from there grew to become a Sommelier in famous restaurants. More recently I have been a Wine Development Manager for the world's second largest wine retailer and I am now Global Wine Buyer for a leading worldwide wine retailer. I spend the year living out of a suitcase blending, tasting and travelling wherever the grapes and vintages take me. My friends hate me. Working in restaurants is where my real love of flavour and wine was nurtured. I loved the job, the showmanship, pace and energy of being a Somm, even if the hours are demanding and my social life was non-existent. It was in fine dining restaurants where I was lucky enough to taste some of the most exquisite and expensive wines and champagnes on Earth. My job was to recommend wines to match with Double Michelin Star food, for ultimate customer satisfaction.

Wine can raise a plate from a forgettable dinner into an occasion, a memorable, taste bud-tantalizing experience. What I love about champagne is the dynamic it brings to a meal. The fizz alters textures, cuts through or combines fats and proteins and lifts flavours to a whole other level. Champagne with food is one of life's true delights.

It wasn't all plain sailing in my restaurant days. I learnt from the bottom up. As my ex-bosses will tell you, I have committed all the faux-pas, the don'ts and never-evers of being a Sommelier and on the whole have tried to learn from my mistakes.

A vivid Somm memory, and one that still makes me cringe, happened in the manic build-up to Christmas 2010. I was serving Krug Vintage 1996 (one of the best champagne Vintages over the last century, with a hefty tag to match) for a table of six, in London's Mayfair. It was a special occasion for the guests, who would over the course of the evening spend thousands of pounds on dinner – and expect the service and execution of the meal to match the expense. The meal was going triumphantly. The aperitifs of dirty martinis and a couple of Negronis had lubricated conversation and the lone olives were waiting patiently in the bottom of the martini glasses. Food ordered, the wine list had been studied and it was time to commit. The discerning selection was made, and the table's spirits were high as the Chef called for their six exquisite, legendary double-baked, two cheese soufflés on a bed of double cream. I had approximately four minutes to fetch their choice bottle from the cool, damp outside cellar, check on and serve two other tables in my restaurant section (a birthday, and an engagement, both at different stages of that season's menu degustation) before the piping hot, cheesy, rich clouds of goodness were served by the lovely Italian waitress. To have the food arrive before the wine in a setting such as that is blasphemous. I wasn't prepared to muddy my Somm reputation that night.

The pace of service was fast, and attention to detail is vital. After ordering the Krug, I stayed on the restaurant floor making sure my guests were well oiled, and looked after the adjoining tables. If you keep in mind that every table could include a Michelin inspector, you remain on your A game. I asked my colleague to fetch the prestige bottle back from the outside cellar for me. Either he was in a mischievous mood, or rushing like hell, either way, when I presented the bottle to the table, and began the delicate opening I didn't realise that the bottle had been shaken up so severely. Instead of the expected gentle pffft from a professional Double Michelin wine waiter opening an older, well-cellared bottle of champagne, I wasn't the only shocked face when the bottle exploded open in my grasp. I instinctively used my hand to dam the aggressive golden fountain shooting literally all over the place, my hand funnelled the spray showering the entire table of six, drowning their dreamy soufflés, and spraying the adjoining couple on their engagement night in hundreds of pounds worth of foaming fizz. I didn't catch a single drop on myself.

Whether you drink your champagne in Michelin-starred restaurants, at home with friends or straight from the bottle at a beach picnic, we all can appreciate the taste, the effervescence and narcotic effect champagne has on us.

Man on a mission

Like many of my generation I was inspired by a young age to try new dishes and explore new cuisines. This passion manifests itself whether I'm munching on an apple, a good bacon roll, or a cheese soufflé. I am from a generation of foodies. It has never been easier to get great, interesting grub: pubs now serve Michelin-starred burgers, and on the high street at lunchtime you're as likely to find authentic Mexican street food as a standard tuna mayonnaise sarnie. I and many of my friends have developed a similar passion in beer. The craft beer scene worldwide has never been so strong, let alone in the UK where you cannot keep up with the heady new flavours of new local microbreweries, it is really exciting to see how fast this category has grown ever since two lads from Aberdeenshire broke the traditional mould. So, have we been inspired in the same way by wine? I don't think we have, yet.

With our colonial legacy, historic trade routes and wealth and diversity of population, Britain has some of the best, most diverse cuisine on our doorsteps. Indian curry is now our national dish, and many of us are more likely to eat pasta during the week than a traditional British dish. But what are we drinking? Just as you would have a squeeze of fresh lemon over your fish to cut through the salty sea flavours with the sharp, sweet, citric twang, wine has the same fresh benefits, and brings more to the party than just a lemon.

We need to bring wine to life. Lots of people would enjoy wine more if it were demystified a little and broken down into simple terms. Wine, and champagne are made to be enjoyed and drunk by everyone, and the smallest amount of knowledge will empower imbibers to make the right choices.

Alongside wine, food has been a passion of mine from my teenage years. Call it greed, or genuine appetite, this spurred a love of flavour. Flavour can change perceptions, incite memories, alter moods, bring people together and divide the best of friends. One of the beauties of flavour is that it is individual, we all taste things differently and have our own ideas as to what we like, and what we don't. Blending wine for a living, I have made a career combining flavours and textures to enhance pleasure, enjoyment and gastronomic experience. I cannot taste for you but I can recommend what I think you, and the wider world of drinkers, will enjoy.

Along the way I'll offer suggestions as to what you might like to eat to both enhance the pleasure of the wine you are drinking and to improve the taste of what you are eating. This book is to add to your drinking and dining experience, and doubles up as a terrific coaster.

Statue of Dom Perignon, Épernay

Origins

To understand the origins of champagne, you need not only to understand the region in North East France, but also the people who drove the creation and evolution of the wine. Champagne wasn't an overnight discovery, but rather developed and evolved over centuries, driven by human endeavour. Many winemakers, entrepreneurs, marketers, and many of those involved have become household names: Dom Pierre Perignon, Jean-Rémy Moët, Dom Ruinart, Widow Clicquot, Charles-Henri Heidsieck to name but a few, who we will meet through this book. Champagne as we know it is close to 300 years old. The first established champagne house was Ruinart in 1729 although champagne was made for sometime before this date, and has gone through drastic changes since.

Early doors

History credits the 17th-century Dom Pierre Perignon with discovering the magic and secret of champagne's bubbles at its now iconic and spiritual home, the Benedictine Abbey of Hautvillers. We have been led to believe that in the dark, damp, chalky cellars, the monk managed to metamorphose the local light, still wine into the sparkling liquid gold wine we know today. However endearing this might be, it couldn't be farther from the truth. Dom Pierre Perignon was certainly an exceptional wine taster, winemaker and grape grower, but he did not manage to capture the magic sparkle of champagne. Dom Perignon's job at Hautvillers Abbey was not to create a new wine but to get rid of the naturally occurring bubbles which were ruining his fellow monks' business in quality still wines. If he had been successful in his job, champagne might have never existed.

If you think Champagne invented sparkling wine you would be wrong. Like many of the best ideas, the invention of champagne wine was a total accident. For the birth of sparkling wines, we must turn to a wee unknown town in the South of France by the name of Limoux.

The first fizz

Limoux is a small, mountain-locked town in the Languedoc-Roussillon area of Mediterranean France, roughly between Toulouse and Montpellier. The first written record of Limoux's Blanquette de Limoux sparkling wine is in 1531 at the abbey of St. Hilaire, but likely the wines had been made for some time previously. At this point champagne didn't even exist. This is over a century before the birth of Dom Perignon. Like champagne and most wines and spirits through Europe at the time, the wines of Limoux were made by the Benedictine monks and the Church. Many of the spectacular monasteries you see across the continent were directly funded by booze. Until the late 1700s the sparkling wines of Limoux and Champagne were made in a similar way to today's artisan cider. After pressing the grapes, natural yeasts found in the winery would begin fermenting the grape juice into wine, converting the sugars of the grapes into alcohol. For fermentation you need a steady, pleasant temperature otherwise the yeasts give up and go dormant, which would happen over the cold winters of 1500s rural France. This meant the wines were bottled even though the fermentation was hibernating during the cold winter months… until Spring came and kickstarted the process again.

There are two main byproducts of a wine's fermentation: alcohol and CO_2 gas. So, come the spring when the weather warmed up the bottles and the yeasts got back to work, the fermentation would carry on, fermenting the rest of the sugars into alcohol and trapping the CO_2 in the bottle, dissolving it into the wine… and voila: sparkling wine. Of course at the beginning this was totally accidental. Glass was not as strong as it is today, so when a monk went down into the cellar in the spring, he would find a lot of his precious wine bottles had exploded. Champagne for a long time was called Devil's Wine, because of the danger associated with the exploding bottles, which has been responsible for many deaths throughout its history. It would take hundreds of years to streamline and develop this process (now called méthode traditionnelle), in the chalk cellars of champagne, making it safe and reliable.

Méthode traditionnelle

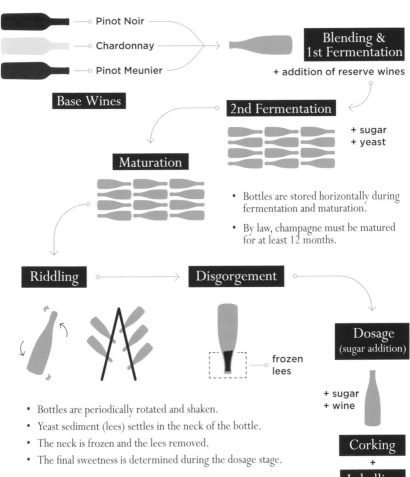

Pinot Noir
Chardonnay
Pinot Meunier

Base Wines

Blending & 1st Fermentation
+ addition of reserve wines

2nd Fermentation
+ sugar
+ yeast

Maturation

- Bottles are stored horizontally during fermentation and maturation.
- By law, champagne must be matured for at least 12 months.

Riddling → **Disgorgement**

frozen lees

Dosage
(sugar addition)
+ sugar
+ wine

Corking
+
Labelling

- Bottles are periodically rotated and shaken.
- Yeast sediment (lees) settles in the neck of the bottle.
- The neck is frozen and the lees removed.
- The final sweetness is determined during the dosage stage.

Sweetness Level	Sugar Content (grams per litre)
Brut Nature	0–3 g/L
Extra Brut	0–6 g/L
Brut	0–12 g/L
Extra Dry	12–17 g/L
Dry	17–32 g/L
Demi Sec	32–50 g/L
Doux	50+ g/L

Getting ready to cork, Pol Roger, Épernay

Steel vats, Pol Roger

Maturing casks, Billecart-Salmon

Making champagne is the most complex, expensive, difficult, time-consuming way to produce wine there is, and it requires an understanding of the region's soils, grape varieties, vineyards and complex production method. This evolution and improvement to techniques has taken hundreds of years to refine and perfect which results in the ultimate quality expression we now find in our champagne glasses.

Before wine is put into the bottle for the start of the méthode traditionelle, a Chef du Cave (head winemaker) may blend 30,000 wines from different areas, vineyards, ages and complexities, to produce a consistent quality-driven wine, which not only showcases the champagne house style, but the vintage and even the personality of the Chef du Cave themselves. This is why, whether you drink Veuve Clicquot today or in 50 years' time, you know that the distinctive orange label guarantees a certain style. Although the champagne may not be made from the exact same vineyards, wine or year, it will be a definitive showcase of the house style, expressing not only the winemaker's signature, but providing a glimpse into the personality of the Widow Clicquot herself.

King and country

Reims Cathedral, in the capital of champagne, stands as tall as Notre Dame in Paris, and is where the first king of France was baptised in the 5th century. And what did they celebrate this event with? The local wines of champagne of course! It became traditional for all the kings and queens of France to be crowned in Reims and this led to a halo effect on the region of champagne, and its wines. If the royal family were seen to be selecting and enjoying the wines of champagne for their special events, those wines became even more desirable.

Louis XV was a known party animal and lover of the finest things, and drank an obscene amount of champagne. He became publicly affiliated with a few of the region's more prominent producers, including Claude Moët who would visit Versailles to sell his wines to the royal court. One of the defining moments in the history of champagne was in 1728, when Louis passed a decree allowing the wines of champagne to be transported in bottles, no doubt a suggestion from Claude himself.

This was a huge step forward in champagne's evolution, as all wine from all other wine regions had to be transported in barrels. Champagne producers could now sell and send finished wine directly to the consumers in France and beyond.

It gave them an opportunity to form their own brands and identity. It had a big effect on the final quality of the wine when it reached the customer, as sealed bottles kept fresher than wines being transported by barrel. This meant champagne became the first wine to be shipped, exported and importantly marketed around the world.

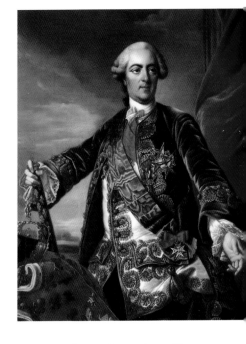

It also affected drinking habits closer to home, including for King Louis XV. The cumbersome task of moving, filling, decanting and serving wine out of a barrel was a thing of the past, with glass bottles being served directly at the dinner table. Louis could banish the serving staff at his lavish parties at Versailles, and serve himself from the bottle. Without the prying eyes of his staff, the king and his guests could get up to much more raucous behaviour.

"Champagne is the only wine that leaves a woman beautiful after drinking it."

— Madame de Pompadour, official mistress to Louis XV

Claude Moët was a man with leverage, by the mid 1700s he was producing more champagne than anyone else in the region. He used his political connections and sublime salesmanship to flog more fine champagne to the royal courts and influencers in France and Europe. This power still holds true, as Moët & Chandon are still the largest champagne house, by some way.

● **Montagne de Reims**
 — Area for Pinot Noir
● **Vallée de la Marne**
 — Area for Pinot Meunier
◯ **Côte des Blancs**
 — Area for Chardonnay

Montagne de Reims

Reims

Vallée de la Marne

Épernay

Châlons-en-Champagne

Côte des Blancs

Sézanne

Côte de Sézanne

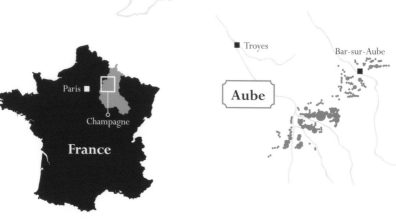

Troyes

Bar-sur-Aube

Paris

Champagne

Aube

France

The region

Champagne has a cool, rather British climate meaning the wine growers of champagne have always had difficulty reaching full ripeness in their grapes. If you're sceptical about climate change, then talk to a champagne vigneron (grape grower) and he'll tell you that annual temperatures are creeping up every year. With wine, the heat of the region translates directly into the style of what's in the final glass. Heat means ripeness, ripeness means sugar, sugar means alcohol. That's why the wines of warmer climates like Australia are dark, jammy, high in booze and full-bodied as the grapes generally reach ripeness before they are harvested.

Historically, in Champagne the opposite happened: the grapes wouldn't be ripe when picked, lacking the sugar, colour, acid and flavour which wine growers generally look for when producing wine. Still wines made from these grapes are thin and very acidic. You could strip paint with the old champagne still wines! But it wasn't all bad news. Due to the wine's high natural acidity, it enabled the wines to last longer in the barrel (all wine was transported in wooden barrels until the 1700s) without spoiling. Just as you would pickle foodstuffs to stop them going off, acid keeps things fresh. Wine producers could then ship their wines further afield, down the Marne River from Champagne to Paris before exporting them to London, the Netherlands and beyond. This was crucial in Champagne's later success. Champagne was competing with other famous wine regions of France, and building a reputation as a quality wine region even though at this point, the wines were still without bubbles. It is what happened next that would change champagne forever.

How the British invented Champagne (nearly)

For the next chapter in the champagne story we must look closer to home, as there is a theory that we Brits are an important piece of champagne's historical jigsaw. In the late 17th century barrels of thin, light, acidic still champagne wines were shipped to the wine merchants, inns and restaurants of London and the rest of the country. What the merchants and barmen did next is very important – they added sugar, and a touch of brandy to the barrels of wine. This had two dramatic effects: firstly it made the wines more friendly, fruitier due to the sweetness and easy to drink, and the brandy helped the wine from going off. This relationship with sweetness was the start of a long love affair between champagne wines and sugar.

Many of the barmen and innkeepers found that adding a touch of sugar to their barrels and bottles made the wine froth and sparkle. At first, this was an undesired effect, but tastes and fashion evolved and it wasn't long before we Brits got a serious thirst for sparkling wines.

In effect, in our efforts to stop the imported wine from going off, we haphazardly stumbled upon the secondary fermentation required to make sparkling wine. So at a time when Dom Perignon was working away in his cellar to rid his wines of the unwanted bubbles, British barmen were working hard to understand how to produce them.

The sparkling wine process didn't stay haphazard for long. An Englishman, Christopher Merret, presented a scientific paper to the Royal Society of London in 1662 in which he explained how adding sugar could produce gentle sparkling in the wines, which took a lot of ideas from an ancient cider-making method. By 1670, it is believed that the UK were bottling and converting their barrelled imported wine from Champagne into sparkling wine, at least ten years before the first desired sparkling wine was produced in France. Controversial, I know! 'Merret' was in fact proposed by Ridgeview, the first English Sparkling producer, to be the name of 'English Sparkling Wine'. It was rejected, but the top quality producer based on the Sussex Downs still produces a Merret Cuvée in tribute to him.

Whether or not the British innkeepers had a role to play, we do know our most important British contribution to champagne was our glassware. Glass in France was expensive and the French didn't have the means to create strong bottles, which was why the glass in the cellars of champagne and Limoux kept shattering. The French glass-blowers used wood fires, whereas their British counterparts used coal, achieving a much higher temperature and thus producing strong, durable bottles robust enough to cope with the pressure from the secondary fermentation.

But, really, we can't take any of the credit. We (us Brits) were ahead of the game in terms of understanding the science behind champagne's secondary fermentation in bottle or méthode traditionelle (which it is now called) but we didn't pursue it. We let the Champenois do what they do best and make champagne. It really wasn't until a local French pharmacist in the 19th century, André François, trialled and discovered the precise measurement of how much sugar is needed to create the sparkle in the bottles, without producing too much pressure, when champagne really became the success story of what it is today. The discoveries of André François meant that production could be streamlined and commercialized. This led to a big bang in production; from a mere 300,000 bottles a year to 20 million by the mid-19th century which led to a greater popularity of the drink. While champagne was still the favoured tipple of the rich, famous and elite, it became more assessable to the everyday drinker and the emerging middle classes. Nowadays, total bottle production of champagne sits around 340 million bottles, and demand still surpasses supply.

Sweet tooth

Over the last 300 years, champagne has gone through many changes – in how the grapes were grown, made, blended and tasted – but there is one constant that links all successful houses and the styles of champagne they produce: they listen to the final drinker. As recently as the 1900s champagne was sickly sweet, and not the dry refreshing style we know today. Brut or Dry was developed for the British consumer, (you'll find more information on this on the Pommery page), after we the consumers told the champagne houses that the champagne was too sweet for us. Champagne was originally drunk as a dessert wine during the 1800s when Russia and America with their very sweet teeth (still true today) were becoming more important as export markets. Champagnes drunk in France at the time had up to two hundred grams of sugar a litre, and Russians liked it with three hundred grams per litre. That champagne would have been almost syrupy in consistency and three times sweeter than Coca Cola, or twice as sweet as most sweet wines. Sauternes, famous sweet wine from Bordeaux, for instance is around 150 grams per litre.

War

Champagne is a region built on conflict and tension, as Richard Geoffroy, Chef du Cave of Dom Perignon explained to me when I sat with him in Dom Perignon's Hautvillers Abbey. Champagne sits on vital trade routes, and this has been a blessing for business, but as it is also a strategically valuable position, pain and war have been common. From Attila the Hun in the 5th century through to Napoleon's war with Russia to the First and Second World Wars, conflict has played as much a part in champagne's history as the grapes themselves.

Both world wars had a dramatic effect on champagne. The outbreak of World War II compromised all champagne production. Following the German invasion there was heavy damage to and looting of Champagne's cellars, a Nazi General was appointed to control champagne solely for the thirsty needs of the German armies. Champagne's intoxicating effects were morale-boosting and uplifting, even for the Nazis, and it was used to incentivize the men. And they needed it, up to 400,000 bottles were sent to the German armies across the continent every week during the war.

Often the champagne sent was of inferior or tempered quality, as the French Resistance was strong in the region, which was often at the front line of battle. Instead of sending their prized bottles, they often sent dish-washer quality, packed in their usual bottles hoping the German army's palates generally wouldn't be discerning enough to know the difference. Certain champagne houses were ordered to give vast quantities to the Nazis, which the Champenois resistance used to their advantage with their British allies. The Resistance were provided with important military intelligence when they started to track the champagne shipments: through the vast orders they could pre-empt where the Germans were preparing to attack next which was of great use during the war.

But, the champagne houses knew that if the Germans kept up their huge thirst for champagne they would literally drink the cellars and region dry. So, in 1941 the Comité Interprofessionnel du Vin de Champagne was established, a collective body which protects, organizes and represents the growers and producers of the region, it was the first of its kind in the world and is just as strong today in protecting the interests of the region and its wines.

This united voice has been so important to all of champagne, bringing producers, brokers and growers together for the common goals of higher quality, increased visibility and the eradication is costly, unnecessary competition. The CIVC traded and negotiated with the Germans, to create a sustainable model of supply. Without them, Champagne would be a very different place, and drink today.

Success story

We need to look to more modern times to understand champagne's real success: Champagne as we know it is a post-war phenomenon. The region had to contend with severe setbacks in the late 19th and early 20th centuries. Phylloxera, a vine louse, ate 99% of all the vines in the region, which meant the entire area had to be replanted and grafted on resistant roots. This devastated the world of wine and its effect can still be felt in the champagne and wine industry now. Some champagne houses (like Louis Roederer and Moët & Chandon) had the foresight to purchase a lot of primely situated vines when the prices were rock bottom. Nowadays, the real estate in Champagne is some of the most expensive land in the world: for a block of vines in the Côte des Blancs you would pay the same price for a penthouse in Manhattan.

Following the wars, two of the largest markets collapsed due to the revolution in Russia and the Prohibition which stopped most sales into America from 1920 until 1933. The enterprising Champenois had to look elsewhere to sell their wines, and the Germans and Brits are still to this day the most important export markets for Champagne. We Brits are by far the most important market, outside of France. In fact, up until a couple of years ago London drank more champagne than the entire United States!

Toasting to victory

"Remember gentlemen, it's not just France we are fighting for, it's Champagne!"
—*Winston Churchill*

On the 7th of May 1945, a week after Hitler's suicide in Berlin, the German command signed the surrender treaty in the cobbled city of Reims, ending the war. The population, including General Dwight Eisenhower and the representatives of the Allied forces present, celebrated with champagne just as the French kings had done for hundreds of years before them. It seemed fitting to bring the war to a close in a place which had shown so much courage, lost so many but remained so strong. As the legendary Jean-Baptiste Lecaillon, the Chef du Cave at Louis Roederer told me:

'We should not forget, we Champenois are survivors, we have survived the fatalities of Europe. We are the poorest region in France and have seen so many horrible things, and the world wars have been fought in our vineyards and towns. This is why they have made wine, to celebrate life and joy, because the Champenois have suffered so much. Celebrating life is ingrained in the DNA of the people, the region and the wines of Champagne.'

So, when you come to pop the cork off your next bottle of champagne, hopefully one of the 50 included here, give a thought to the people behind the best drink on earth, and don't only toast with champagne, but to Champagne and the Champenois. Cheers!

CELLIER
SIR WINSTON CHURCHILL

Pol Roger, Épernay

Riddling racks, Charles Heidsieck cellars, Reims

The four pillars of taste

Overarching the different styles of champagne are four pillars which are part of every bottle of bubbly; Acid, Toast, Fizz and Sweetness.

Acid

The primary characteristic of wine which contributes to wine's tart and sharp flavours, and is the backbone of all champagne. Acid and acidic are words the wine trade likes to mask when talking to customers, as it doesn't sound very appealing. Instead we (the wine trade) often use words like fresh, crisp, refreshing, vibrant, lively, clean and bright. If you see any of these words on wine labels, they are referring to acidity, which is a good thing.

Toast ▮

I have given every champagne within these pages a Toast Factor, you won't find this anywhere else. I believe one of the most important aspects of champagne and whether or not you like or dislike a champagne is down to its 'toastiness'. This refers to autolysis, which gives champagne its unique flavour and creamy texture. The more time champagne has in contact with its lees, which are the reductive breakdown of yeast cells within a maturing bottle of champagne following secondary fermentation… means the more flavour of toast, brioche, nougat, nuts, shortbread, biscuits, croissants, caramel, toffee and cream (I could go on) the champagne will have. These flavours are exclusive to champagne, and your enjoyment will be dictated whether or not Toast flavours are desirable to you or not. I, for one, bloody love them.

Fizz!

Champagne's calling card. Built up from the secondary fermentation in bottle, fizz is what makes champagne so special. We all love bubbles – look at the world's obsession with soft drinks – and champagne was the first popularized fizzy drink on the planet. No other drink on earth has such associations with bubbles. The bubbles carry flavour and alcohol, each champagne bottle will contain approximately 49 million bubbles, if in doubt you can count them yourself.

Sweetness levels

Note: The official sweetness levels can be found on page 9. The historic system dictates grams of sugar per litre. As most champagne bottles are 75cl, I have listed these sweetness levels in their per bottle equivalent.

Brut Nature / Zero Dosage / Ultra Brut

Rare to find and razor sharp, bone dry at around 2 grams of sugar per bottle. Generally favoured by real champagne lovers, as it is more austere due to the low sugar level. Mostly made by champagne houses who want to showcase the flavour and style of the fruit and terroir, there is little added sugar to mask any impurity. These champagnes can age very well, if you can find them!

Extra Brut

Dry, less than 4.5 grams of sugar per bottle. Like Brut Nature these styles are generally made by quality-focussed producers unlike the mass-market styles. These are some of my personal favourite styles.

Brut

By far the most popular style of champagne and made by most producers. Brut champagnes will carry up to 9 grams of sugar per bottle which means there will be a touch of sweetness in every glass.

Extra Sec / Extra Dry

A rare, off-dry style which carries 9-13 grams of sugar per bottle, most producers will just make a Brut style.

Sec

Medium-sweet style, a rarity which carries between 13-24 grams of sugar per bottle, delicious with cheese.

Demi-Sec

Perfect for puddings. Sweet, fizzy, delicious with up to 37.5 grams of sugar per bottle.

Doux

Very rare, very sweet. A nod back to the original styles of champagne with more than 37.5 grams of sugar per bottle. These are like drinking cream soda and lemonade.

Champagne styles

Blanc de Blancs

100% Chardonnay, a white grape. Literally, a white wine from white grapes, these styles are often fresher and lighter and more lemony than champagnes made with other styles. And if aged tend to be toastier.

Blanc de Noirs

100% from black grapes; Pinot Noir and Pinot Meunier, one or the other or a blend of the two. This style tends to be fuller in the mouth, often rounder and shows more red apple and red berry character.

NV, Non-Vintage (Multi-Vintage)

By far the most popular and widely available of all champagne styles, accounting for 90% of all production. These are a blend of multiple vintages of champagne, and can include all the champagne grapes. By blending multiple vintages together houses can produce consistent styles of their NVs year after year to maintain house style and consistency of quality. NV champagnes have to age for a minimum of 15 months on lees before release, but are often aged a lot longer. As these styles will make up the lion's share of any champagne house's production, it is even more important for houses to create the best champagne they can as NV.

Vintage

Vintage champagne must contain 100% of single harvest, and only be made in exceptional years. Champagne houses on average will only produce vintage champagnes six years out of 10, which is increasingly due to the increased fair weather and global warming, and is at the sole discretion of the Chef du Cave. These individual styles must be aged for a minimum of 36 months in the cellar before release, but houses will often age for an extended period depending on the required style. Vintage champagne only accounts for a small proportion of total production, and is often the most expensive and desirable due to the shorter supply. You will find some crackers in the following pages...

Rosé

Rosé, or pink champagne can be made one of two ways; either leaving the juice in contact with the black skins of Pinot Noir and/or Meunier to extract colour and flavour. Or a proportion of red wine can be blended in with the clear to produce the desired style and colour. All champagne grape juice is clear when pressed, so all the colour comes from the skins. This is exactly the same principle as red wines.

Prestige Cuvées

These are the top expression of champagne houses, and often the most expensive. Styles and methods can vary between houses; some are single vineyard wines or 'Clos', many are vintage declarations, while some are multi-vintage blends from the top years. It totally depends on the house style and what they believe to be their ultimate expression. These champagnes often see extended ageing before release and can age for years, gaining richness and developing complexity. Prestige Cuvées are always the ultimate style of the house.

Davy examines the sediment, Pol Roger

Pol Roger's most important Prestige Cuvées

Classification

Champagne is the largest wine region with a single appellation in France, within this appellation however there are two important classifications. When you read 'Grand' or 'Premier Cru' in regards to champagne, or other French wines, it refers to the original quality classification of the region. In Champagne this system was originally developed to set prices for the best quality grapes from the different village areas. Due to the labour, cash and time investment needed to make champagne it meant most vineyard growers in the region would choose to sell their crop to large champagne houses, as opposed to making champagne themselves. This market dynamic between grape grower and champagne house has sculpted the industry as we know it today. Depending on where vines are planted it drastically affects the price a farmer can charge for his crop. For Grand Cru sites – the best quality areas – farmers could charge 100% of the set price, 90>99% for Premier Cru, and anything the market commands for the village quality of under 90%.

Grand Cru

If you see this on a label, it means business. This designates the best class of vineyards in the whole of champagne. Out of 319 listed villages in the region only 17 have this Grand status. These wines will be the most sought after by large houses for blending components, as they tend to be the most flavoursome and long-lasting. If Grand Cru is written on a label it means 100% of that wine has come from a Grand Cru site.

Premier Cru

This is the second best class of villages in the region. 42 out of the 319 have Premier Cru status, and like Grand Cru it means 100% of the wine must come from a Premier Cru village. Some of these wines are of parallel quality to their Grand Cru partners but not always. And wines will be better priced because of it.

But be assured, for champagnes which don't carry Grand or Premier Cru it doesn't mean they are of substandard quality, but rather fall outside the original quality classification. For instance, Dom Perignon is sourced predominantly from Grand Cru vineyards, but also the Premier Cru vineyard of Hautvillers Abbey, which only makes up a small percentage – but legally means Dom Perignon cannot be labelled as Grand Cru. It's all or nothing.

Seven factors of flavour

Vineyard

Where the vines are grown directly affects the flavour of the grapes, resulting in different expressions in your glass. Soils, altitude and aspects of the elements and sun affects the ripening and quality of the finished champagne. The best quality vineyards are classified as Grand or Premier Cru which generally indicates a higher level of chalk, resulting in the best quality champagnes. Chalk is champagne's calling card, it means grapes can reach full ripeness of sugar and flavour, whilst retaining high acidity and low pH. This translates into wines with full flavour whilst retaining great freshness and longevity. Another important factor in finished quality of champagne is the yield at harvest; if a grape grower can harvest 18 tons of grapes per hectare of vines, the quality and concentration will be diluted compared to a grower producing smaller yields, resulting in more concentration and flavour in the finished wine. Organic and biodynamic vineyards produce some of the smaller yields, and more flavoursome grapes.

Vintage

Wine is an agricultural product, and grapes can only be produced once a year. Many factors throughout an annual growing cycle affect the vine and final quality of the grapes picked at harvest. Vintage variation is particularly poignant in cool climate regions like Champagne. If it is a particularly hot year the grapes will be riper, have sweeter flavours, more sugar and less acidity which will taste very different to a cool year, where the wines will have higher acid & more tart fruit flavours. Champagne is often made as a multi-vintage blend or non-vintage blend in order to mitigate these vintage variations, to create a more consistent style. Vintages are a celebration of a specific year, and are generally only produced in good or great years.

Blend

Champagne can be made with six grape varieties grown in the region. But three grapes; red grapes Pinot Noir, Pinot Menier and white grape Chardonnay are by far the most important, each making up a third of the region's planting. Each grape carries a different flavour, and the proportions used will give different flavours. Blends of the three grapes are the most common, but blanc de blancs made from white wines and blanc de noirs made exclusively from red grapes are also important.

Time

Champagne is bottled time. Each non-vintage style you find has a minimum of 15 months' ageing, but often will have a lot longer. Vintage champagne has a minimum of 36 months before release, while Prestige Cuvées often have up to six years' ageing. Generally, the older aged champagnes will have more toast and nutty flavours, the younger fresher and fruitier ones.

Style & Sweetness

Whether it is Brut, Extra Brut, Demi Sec or Doux etc. these styles of champagne will dictate the sweetness, and we all have a varied sweet tooth. 90% of all champagne is made in a Brut style, which translates to less than a gram of sugar in your glass.

House

Each champagne producer has their own house style, just as each of us have our own style of cooking or dress sense. Many house styles have been honed down and whittled over hundreds of years, some have developed or changed their style more recently. Both history and the Chef du Cave (Champagne winemaker) dictate the style which they make each year, and many Chefs will follow a similar recipe every year to achieve consistency. Reserve wines are a house's secret weapon and how they use, age and mature their reserve wines drastically affects the flavour of what's in your glass. Reserve wines can be aged in oak, steel or even in bottle and can be up to 20 or 30 years old by the time they are blended into the new champagne. Many houses produce similar styles but the best houses have their own unique approach, which both separates them from the competition and links the champagnes they produce.

Tasting with Chef du Cave, Cyril Brun

Fizz with food

Food and wine matching still isn't taken very seriously in the UK, an afterthought at best, but if you follow a few simple principles it can lift a mundane meal and glass of wine into a gastronomic extravaganza whatever the occasion, so please pay attention.

There are books and books on the principles of food and wine matching; you could write a bloody dissertation on it – I did! But as any Sommelier will tell you, you can't learn anything without trial and error, and you can't do this without eating, drinking and evaluating.

On the most basic level, food and wine matching serves one purpose; to enhance enjoyment of what you are eating and drinking.

To dig slightly deeper, it is to enhance enjoyment of what you are eating and drinking by combining or contrasting the tastes and flavours of a dish to the wine, whilst utilizing taste attributes of a dish (sweetness, bitterness, acidity, astringency, saltiness) to bring out desired flavours in both food and wine. For two reasons:

1. Balance. If a food and wine match is good it should be balanced, that means you can taste everything from the dish and wine harmoniously, making it even more delicious.
2. Gusto. A good food and wine match should create more flavour and more taste for the diner i.e. combining the wine and food means you get more out of each component on the plate or in the glass than you would when you taste them separately. This means a food and wine match will taste better than the sum of its parts; $1+1=3$ so to speak.

The fundamental difficulty with food and wine matching is the unknown of what the wine will taste like, and the risk of parting with money for an unknown isn't appealing. If you are buying a bottle from the supermarket shelf or wine shop, unless you know the wine it is near impossible to know exactly how it's going to taste, even if you do read the back label. This is the role of the Sommelier; to match the desired flavour of a wine to the customer's wants, to enhance the plate of food which the chef has cooked, in budget for the customer. Champagne with the correct food is bliss. It shouldn't be forgotten that champagne is a wine and has all the same elements as the still variety. Champagne is usually opened as an aperitif – after we finish our flute, and eat one too many canapés, we tend to move on to other wines. But why stop the party there?

Pre-dinner is the classic time to open champagne, ironic given that when champagne first became popular it was usually served with dessert. Convention now dictates champagne before dinner for two reasons. First, it gets you buzzed quicker, as the alcohol bursting in the bubbles enters your bloodstream faster than through your stomach lining, you'll know this if you've ever done a flaming Sambuca shot... And secondly, champagne stimulates taste buds: the acidity and bitterness of champagne make you salivate, so it actually makes you thirstier and hungrier.

Champagne brings a fresh dynamic to any meal because, unlike all still wines, it is fizzy. This fizz brings texture in the form of mousse, which often carries a level of astringency and bitterness which, paired with rich or salty flavours, makes for a delicious combination.

Acidity is one of champagne's key pillars, and hugely desirable for food and wine matches, as acidity brings freshness. If you are eating fatty or salty foods, like a deep-fried Mars bar or even a cheese toastie, you need acidity to balance the heaviness and richness of texture and flavour from the fat. We use acidity like this every day, for example malt vinegar on your chips.

Champagne also brings sweetness and we like sugar; our minds are genetically trained to enjoy sweetness. This level of sweetness, paired with the acidity, means champagne is an incredibly versatile food companion. If your dish is salty a touch of sweetness in your wine can work wonderfully well. For example; a fatty, salty cheeseburger benefits from sweet and acidic tomato ketchup. Champagne brings the same principle to any dish.

Champagne's other unique quality is its flavour. Unlike any other wine, champagne's production method gives rise to flavours not found in any other wine, toastiness. This delicious flavour spectrum brings a different element to any plate of food, and like bread it goes well with just about anything. Whether it is soup, starter, main course or dessert, champagne can be drunk with them all.

Two things to keep in mind when choosing your champagne to pair with your meal: age and style. Generally, the older a champagne, the richer and fuller it is going to be. This means an older champagne can be paired with a more wholesome, richer dish.

Charles Heidsieck have created their own
Tulip glass to best show off their cuvées

Know your glasses

If you really want to get maximum enjoyment out of your champagne, it helps to have proper glassware. Don't get me wrong, you can enjoy wine or champagne out of any cup, glass or ski boot. I have even seen it drunk from a protein shaker. If you are a purist, you may like it straight from the bottle. But as long as we have had champagne, we have had a variety of champagne drinking vessels.

We can track the timeline of champagne through its drinking vessels. The shapes and sizes shifted to follow changes in drinking status, trends and fashions, and with an improved understanding of the flavour of champagne. Generally speaking champagne glasses are trying to enhance and accentuate a particular organoleptic quality found in the wine, whilst keeping your hot hands away from the liquid to mitigate the immediate transfer in temperature, and warming your delicately cooled champagne. This is why wine glasses have long stems. But back in the 1700s champagne was often cloudy and the glassware of the time was short, thick and squat enough to hide the murky shades found in the glass. Nowadays, we want to see what we are drinking.

There are three main reasons in the choice of the shape of glass:

1. **Air**. And the ratio of oxygen to wine. The more surface of the wine exposed, the more aromas and smells are released. A fine balance is needed, as too much oxygen can let all the bubbles escape too quickly and allows the aromas to disappear too easily.
2. **Shape**. The shape of the glass will channel aromas and smells in the right direction, i.e. up your schnoz. The shape of the glass will also dictate the persistence and display of bubbles: the narrower and taller the glass, the smaller the ration of air to wine, thus keeping the bubbles alive for longer. The taller the glass, the greater to showboat those cheeky bubbles rising to the frothy surface.
3. **Style**. Champagne is a symbol of status. If you drive a Rolls Royce, you park it where people can see it. If you drink champagne, a lot of people want everyone to know they are drinking champagne. This has been the case since champagne came to market in the 1600s when people wanted to clearly

Spicy Red

Bold Red/
Bordeaux Glass

Aromatic Red/
Burgundy Glass

Light White

Bold White

One Size Fits All

Tulip (sparkling)

Flute (sparkling)

Coupe (sparkling)

Sweet Fortified

Sweet White

Dry Fortified

Any of these glass shapes can be used for drinking champers. I'd recommend the tulip or light white glass for everyday use, and a bold white glass for older champagnes.

differentiate social groups drinking. The best way to do this is to waft and wave your coupes or flutes around the place, or hope your Sommelier showers you and the restaurant with it!

The most famous of champagne's glasses has to be the shallow coupe, said to be modelled on the breasts of France's queen, Marie Antoinette. Although this glass was actually created specifically for sparkling wine in England in the 1690s, I still like to think Marie Antionette's desirable bosom had a part to play in the design. There have been a few modern versions of the famous glass, courtesy of Dom Perignon and Kate Moss. But luckily for us, no other royal family has been asked to mould a glass. The coupe became hugely popular in the UK, the States and Russia, glamorized by champagne houses, including Veuve Clicquot. A big selling point in the UK was that the glass looked like it contained more champagne! Good for the houses, as they sold more bottles.

However fun they are to use, the problem with the coupe glass for drinking champagne is the shape: although breast-like, it is too short and too wide. This means, once poured, the champagne goes flat a little too quickly. Nowadays, coupe glasses are used to serve older styles of champagne, but you are more likely to have a cocktail served in one, than a glass of bubbly.

Flutes are popular because they showcase the teeny, gently rising bubbles up the narrow sides of a tall, elegant glass, thus continuing champagne's visual appeal. The best flutes have etching in the bottom of the glass to act as a nucleation point for the steady, even stream of bubbles. Another major plus for the flute (from personal experience) is that it's much harder to spill your precious fizz due to the physics of the taller sides of the glass. I wasn't very good at physics, but the more science can help us when drinking the better.

But there's been another shift in times, and it is time to say farewell to the flutes. I hate them! Although flutes are visually pleasing, they do not best showcase the quality of champagne in the glass, in fact they impede it. Like fine wine, there is a certain amount of oxygen needed to open and aerate the aromas and flavours, and flutes don't do this. The shape of the flute inhibits the style, and can hide flavour. For me, I'm happier drinking my Champers out of white wine or normal wine glasses. This means I can gorge on the style and fully appreciate the aromas and tastes released in the glass. I recommend you follow suit.

Many of the top champagne houses have devised bespoke glasses for their own top cuvées. When I visited Dom Perignon, we tasted (drank) out of bulb-shaped glasses with a tapered lip, more similar to Burgundy glasses made for red wine. The perfect glass for champagne was devised between head Sommelier in Reims' top Michelin restaurant, Les Crayères and the town's university. The result is a tulip-shaped glass which offers the best of both flutes and wine glasses. Basically, the glass is made to respect the role of the mousse or effervescence found in the champagne, which carries more intensity of flavour than the liquid itself. The shape of the tulip glass gives more air to the surface of the champagne, thus allowing more of the fizzy aromas to escape, then cleverly tapers around the rim to allow each one of the bubbles to burst simultaneously at the glass's widest point. So, when you stick your nose in for a whiff, you get maximum flavour and aromas from the bursting champagne bubbles. BOOM!

Even Riedel, the world's most premium and famous glass producer, still make flutes for commercial demand, but advise drinkers to drink champagne from a wine-shaped glass. So, next time you pop a cork, do yourself a favour and use a proper glass.

Bottle sizes

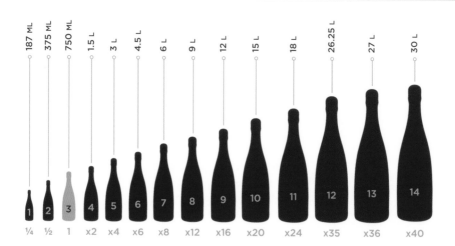

1 **Quart** 187 ml

2 **Demi** 375 ml ——————————— equals ½ Standard Bottle

3 Standard Bottle 750 ml

4 **Magnum** 1.5 l

5 **Jéroboam** 3 l

6 **Réhoboam** 4.5 l ——————————— equals **6** Standard Bottles

7 **Methusaleh** 6 l

8 **Salmanazar** 9 l

9 **Balthazar** 12 l ——————————— equals **16** Standard Bottles

10 **Nebuchadnezzar** 15 l

11 **Solomon** 18 l

12 **Sovereign** 26.25 l

13 **Primat** 27 l

14 **Melchizedek** 30 l ——————————— equals **40** Standard Bottles

Price index

Champagne is expensive! It is part of the allure. Although you find it in supermarkets under £10 nowadays it is worth a lot more. Supermarkets will use champagne to drive footfall into their stores, and will often make a loss on the champagnes they sell to draw customers in to spend money on other things. I have not included any champagnes which drive this behaviour, and most of the champagnes I have included won't sell for much under £20. Champagnes are often heavily discounted by retailers, especially over the festive period where most stores sell the vast majority of their annual sales in the six weeks in the run-up to Christmas and New Year.

I have based my pricing guide on the average bottle price as:

  ££ Under £30
  £££ Between £30 and £50
  ££££ Between £50 and £100
  £££££ Over £100

The champagnes

The distinctive André Clouet labels were designed by
Jean-François Clouet's great-grandfather in 1911

André Clouet

I came late to the wines of André Clouet, but boy am I now an avid believer. Current proprietor Jean-François makes his wines in his ancestral home and winery in the heartland of champagne's most prized Pinot Noir vineyards in the Grand Cru villages of Ambonnay and Bouzy. His family have been guardians of these vines since the 1400s and making wine since the time Dom Perignon was trying to figure out how to get started. The elaborate, fabulous labels were designed by his great-grandfather in 1911, a nod to the family's printing firm which used to print books for the French kings. But despite this richly-textured history the wines are at the forefront of style and modern champagne, showing vineyard expression, low sweetness and are dripping with personality. These wines are serious expressions of some of the most special vineyards and terroir of Pinot in the world, so if you do open a bottle, make sure you finish it!

Respect for the pure chalk vineyards is key for Jean-François, and his wines are a true reflection of the incredible terroir in which his Pinot Noir grows. These wines are difficult to get hold of and are like gold dust for champagne addicts.

...despite this richly-textured history, the wines are at the forefront of style and modern champagne

Considering the small production, price and unbelievable quality of André Clouet's wines, I believe that when the mass champagne market comes to know the value of Clouet's wines, these champagnes will all become collectors' items and even more difficult to buy. So, stay ahead of the game!

André Clouet
Grand Cru Grande Réserve Brut

01

Tasting notes: Prune brandy, red apple compote and winter spiced tarte tatin on the nose, gorgeous. Inviting and seductive with bags of red fruit, and charred pineapple flavours in the mouth, with some chalky salinity bringing freshness. Seamless cloud-like mousse.

Made from 40-year-old vines from chalky soils of the 100% Grand Cru vineyards of Bouzy and Ambonnay, this magnificent champagne has spent six years resting under the Clouet's 17th-century family home until it was ready for release. Multi-Vintage champagnes only need 15 months' legal ageing before release, so Clouet has gone far beyond the legal requirement. This is expensive for small producers, as a lot of their money is tied up in stock. But for a quality operation like Clouet, he goes the extra mile in the quest for quality.

TYPE Multi-Vintage Brut, Blanc de Noirs

STYLE Iron fist in a velvet glove

PRICE 🍷🍷

STOCKISTS Specialist

TOAST 🍞🍞🍞

FOOD Fried chicken and sticky rice

OCCASION Family reunion (if you like your family)

André Clouet
Jour de 1911

Tasting notes: Complex, wine-like and ludicrously attractive. Pruney too with burnt apple crumble and vanilla custard on the nose. A delicious touch of funk, with a wild honey and waxy edge to the palate framed by waves of golden apple flavours, jasmine and tropicana style fruit. Delicious, silky but pretty serious, super mineral and chalky which takes the flavours on and on in the mouth… ending with a marmite-on-toast intensity.

This is a multi-vintage expression of Jean-François's top selection of his best plots in Bouzy. A blend of vintages, 50% of which are from 2002, an epic vintage, and the other half from reserve wines which Jean-François keeps in a solera system, a method of fractional blending to gain complexity, similar to how the Andalusians make sherry. The 2002 component was fermented in Sauternes barrels, which is a sweet wine from Bordeaux. This gives an incredible depth of flavour and preserved sweetness to the blend. Only 1911 bottles are ever produced of this exceptional champagne, and it could sell for four times the price. It gives ANY top Prestige Cuvée a run for its money, so get online NOW and buy some, before I do.

TYPE Multi-Vintage Brut, Blanc de Noirs

STYLE Fizzy eccentric complexity

PRICE ⓔⓔⓔ

STOCKISTS Specialist

TOAST ■■■

FOOD Roast ham with Coca Cola glaze and spiced lentils, or some funky cheese

OCCASION Something worth remembering, like your wedding night

AR Lenoble

champagne-arlenoble.com

Noble by name, and by nature, this brother and sister team produce dignified wines in their boutique operation based in Damery in the heartland of the Vallée de la Marne. The classy wee House is one of the smallest in all Champagne, producing under 400,000 bottles, a fraction compared to the Grande Marques which dominate high street shelves. What they don't have in quantity, owners Anne and Antoine Malassagne make up for in creative and expressive quality which rivals any big player in Champagne. AR Lenoble is one of the very few champagne houses to be consistently family owned and run since its origins in the 1920s. Over this 100-year period their focus and philosophy has changed slightly, as you would expect, but their unfaltering search for quality has never been quenched.

Expressing and caring for their own and diverse vineyards is key for the family. They own vines in the Grand Cru area of Chouilly for Chardonnay, Premier Cru Pinot Noir in Bisseuil and Meunier in their hometown village of Damery. They farm the vines almost organically, in order to nurture as much biodiversity and health in the vineyards as possible to increase naturally lower yields. They even keep bees which encourages pollination in the vineyards and are also an important emblem for the house. They now make honey from the vineyard bees, which is just as sought after as their champagne!

The AR Lenoble team have forged an ambitious and quality-focused reputation over the last few years and I love their approach to their wine styles. Nothing is written in stone, nothing is done because 'It's always been done that way' and they don't have shareholders to keep happy, just their customers and themselves. They adapt their approach to best suit the vintage and are constantly experimenting to get the best style and expression from their vines. Considering the small scale of the operation, the high demand and quality of the wines, AR Lenoble could be charging a lot more for their champagnes. For me they are in a select, forward-thinking group with Selosse and Jacquesson who are making the most exciting wines in the whole of champagne right now. Keep watching this space.

AR Lenoble
Premier Cru Blanc de Noirs 2009

Tasting notes: Generous and intense red cherry, white pepper dance on the mousse with punnets of wild strawberries bursting on the palate. This is a special style of champagne, unique to the Pinot vines of Bisseuil which boogie with the oak flavours of cocoa and vanilla frappuccino which give a perceived sweetness, although sugar is at 3 grams a bottle. The freshness is grapefruit and salty, carrying the flavours on and on with a beautiful chalky salinity. When you get round to popping this beauty open, make sure you don't serve it too chilled as you'll mask its lavishness and don't drink it out of bloody flutes.

Made exclusively from Pinot Noir in the Premier Cru town of Bisseuil. 28% of the blend has been in oak, either vinified in small oak barrels or aged in large oak barrels. This impacts on the flavour of the finished champagne, but also the texture. The oxygen which slowly percolates through the oak barrels gives roasted coffee and vanilla flavours, and also a silkiness and smoothness of texture. This particular style of champagne needs a little time to really show its true colours, so I would recommend cellaring a couple of years to show this wine's potential.

TYPE Vintage Brut, Blanc de Noirs

STYLE Foaming strawberry opulence

PRICE £££

STOCKISTS Specialist

TOAST 🍞🍞🍞

FOOD Monkfish curry with coconut rice

OCCASION It's your birthday!

Steps leading to the main tasting area within Charles Heidsieck's cellars, 30 metres below ground

Carving in the chalk walls of Heidsieck's cellars,
probably dating back to the 18th century

Armand de Brignac

armanddebrignac.com

When Shawn 'Jay Z' Carter bought Armand de Brignac Champagne in 2014 after he made the owners an offer they 'simply couldn't refuse', the Ace of Spades Champagne became the number one choice of champagne to the rapper's delight. This purchase was in total retaliation after the CEO of Louis Roederer who makes Jay Z's old fave Cristal Champagne publicly stated that he did not want any endorsements from the rap star. So Jay Z did what rappers do best, one-upped him by buying his own champagne house: no one is going to diss the boss.

The champagne style is immediate and rich

It was first endorsed by Jay Z in 2006 when the blingin bottle was shot in his music video Show Me What You Got, since then it has been the choice tipple of gangsters, Wall Street Bankers, celebrities and wannabes. You've got to admit, it looks the part! A city trader famously racked up over £200,000 on a night club bar tab in London, which included the most expensive bottle of champagne in the world: the 30-litre bottle of Ace of Spades,

at a casual £125,000 a pop. They probably charged him for mixer, knowing the clubs in London.

Fancy bars and nice restaurants is where you drive desirability and brand visibility. This is a champagne which was created for the desired market, and it's done beautifully well. The champagne style is immediate and rich, perfect for any occasion; on a yacht in St Tropez or in a basement in Soho this fizz will deliver. The clever marketing and way-over-the-top design looks fantastic in your ice bucket.

This champagne is the epitome of the glamorous and ostentatious lifestyle with which champagne is often associated, but which only a select few get to live. Champagne is champagne because of the varied styles, the spread of price points and the diversity of drinkers who enjoy champagne for their own reasons. Each bottle carries a different message to the drinker, and whether you want to buy champagne as a status symbol in a club, to truly savour for the sake of flavour, or to enjoy the experience rather than the drink with loved ones, it doesn't matter. The champagne's aura and glamour fizzes and foams down every single bottle if you are lucky enough to open one.

Armand de Brignac
Brut Gold

Tasting notes: Stone fruit, ripe and juicy with bags of blinging red cherry and candied citrus, peaches and cream. The palate is ripe and exotic with an array of vanilla, passion fruit and honey flavour which twerks with freshness. The fizz is gentle and foaming, which leaves you heading to the dance floor, or asking for more.

Cattier's flagship champagne is a blend of 40% Pinot Noir, 40% Chardonnay and 20% Pinot Meunier, this is a rich but friendly style of champagne which offers complexity for discerning drinkers, and generosity for people who just want to enjoy it! If you have some money to burn...

TYPE Prestige Cuvée, Multi-Vintage Brut

STYLE Peaches and cream

PRICE £££££

STOCKISTS Specialist

TOAST 🍞🍞🍞

FOOD Roasted quail, or caviar in your limo

OCCASION YOLO

Billecart-Salmon

champagne-billecart.fr

There are few champagne houses which live up to the modest brilliance of Billecart-Salmon. For this family-run property everything is done to exacting standards with no compromise, and has been for the last 200 years. The current owners are 6th generation Antoine and François who taste every day at 11:30 with their father Jean Roland-Billecart. At the sprightly age of 93, he has over 70 vintages of experience! Paired with a razor-sharp palate, and incredible expertise of the region and terroir means he is still the boss in the blending room and constantly challenges the young guns on their blends!

...they only accept the crème de la crème

Winemaking and quality is paramount to this House, and, unlike a few of its competitors, advertising and marketing campaigns are at the bottom of the priority list. This medium-sized house is located in Mareuil-sur-Aÿ, in the Marne district of champagne. In many ways Billecart-Salmon is intertwined in this small town, with the historical family home, manicured French garden, winery and temperature-controlled barrel room interconnected by chalk cellars beneath the boulevards.

Unlike many houses, Billecart's production is small compared to the amount of wine they vinify each year, selection is meticulous which means they only accept the crème de la crème and sell off the grapes and wine they do not think are worthy to the House's range, so you will undoubtedly be drinking B class Billecart when you drink some of the other more famous Grande Marques.

The winery is spankers, not a drop or drip out of place which already evokes the clean and correct wine styles of the House. In 1952 Billecart were the first to pioneer cold settling of the grape juice before fermentation, a technique which is now used all over Champagne, giving clarity and fruitiness to the final wine style. This process was years ahead of its time, and the inspiration came from a family member who brewed beer! This technique is expensive and time consuming, but for Billecart only the best is good enough.

Billecart-Salmon
Brut Réserve

Tasting notes: Complex and layered in style with dangerous drinkability. Fruits of red apple, white cherry and ripe pears and arranged perfectly with air-light panna cotta and mineral refreshment.

A blend of the three different champagne grapes, including a large proportion of Pinot Meunier, which is often overshadowed by its regal brothers Chardonnay and Pinot Noir. Over a third of the blend comes from reserve wines, which add extra richness of the palate and careful ageing in the peace and quiet of the Billecart's cellars until the time is right for release.

TYPE Multi-Vintage Brut

STYLE Harmonic fruity brightness

PRICE £ £ £

STOCKISTS High street

TOAST 🍞🍞

FOOD You could very easily drink a bottle on its own! Chicken thighs roasted with lemons and shallots would go down a treat

OCCASION Fridays

Billecart-Salmon
Brut Rosé

Tasting notes: A bouquet of cherry blossom, plums and red fruit hail from the glass. This iconic rosé is a light and elegant style, which can be confused for a white champagne when tasted blind. Long and precise with freshness and raspberry charm, this champagne is dangerously moreish.

Another blend of the three champagne varieties. A splash of 7% red Pinot Noir in the blend gives this wine its delicate Salmon pink hue, and elegant red fruit character. This champagne tastes best young, so if you are lucky enough to chance a bottle, grab your lover and drink it!

TYPE Multi-Vintage Rosé

STYLE Romantic prowess

PRICE 🍷🍷🍷

STOCKISTS High street

TOAST 🍞

FOOD Mezze platter or sushi

OCCASION Valentine's, baby!

Billecart-Salmon
Cuvée Sous Bois

Tasting notes: Golden and rich and slightly over the top! This champagne is complex with spice and mouth filling texture obtained from the time in French oak barrel, more 'wine' like than any other champagne I've tasted. Vanilla, wood and ripe white cherry and peaches dance on the palate with butterscotch and foaming cream, remaining fresh and elegant. Wow!

This unique champagne is entirely vinified in oak, like a fine white Burgundy. Another blend of all three main champagne grapes, it has been carefully blended after spending six months in Billecart-Salmon's temperature-controlled barrel room. Sous Bois directly translates as 'under wood' and you can taste it. Forget subtlety, this is unashamedly oaked in style. You can taste the spice, vanilla and butterscotch from the barrel. Billecart's signature elegance and drinkability mean this wine is distinctive and rich. Don't serve too cold, or you will lose the complexity.

TYPE Multi-Vintage Brut

STYLE Over the top

PRICE 🄴🄴🄴

STOCKISTS Specialist

TOAST ▮▮▮▮

FOOD Slow-cooked pulled pork and crunchy apple and beetroot slaw, and sweet potato mash

OCCASION Sunday get-togethers

Vines at dawn, Champagne

Bollinger

champagne-bollinger.com

❧

> "I drink it when I'm happy and when I'm sad. Sometimes I drink it when I'm alone. When I have company I consider it obligatory. I trifle with it if I'm not hungry and drink it when I am. Otherwise I never touch it – unless I'm thirsty"
>
> *– Lilly Bollinger, The Daily Mail, 1961*

Being family owned means decisions at Bollinger are made for the right reasons, i.e. quality, rather than keeping investors happy (as you may find in other large branded champagne houses). Bollinger and Louis Roederer are the last two remaining Grande Marques which still have independent ownership. Good on them!

Every blend has at least 60% Pinot Noir which is the definitive style of the House. Two thirds of fruit comes from their own vineyards which is exclusive for a Grande Marques house of its size – again Roederer is the only other. Centred in the town of Ay, home of the best Pinot Noir in the region, 85% of Bollinger's vineyards are Premier or Grand Cru. The best vineyards give the best grapes, which give the best results in your glass.

Bollinger first appeared in Ian Fleming's work in *Diamonds are Forever* published in 1956, as Her Majesty's Secret Service could only choose the most 'British' of champagnes. Note the Royal Warrant on Bollinger's bottle, granted in 1884 by Queen Victoria who was quite the fan of Bolly. This royal relationship survives to this day as it's said that the Queen loves a splash of Special Cuvée from her own private stash.

'Bollinger? If it's '69, you were expecting me.'

– James Bond, Moonraker, 1979

On screen, it wasn't until 1973 in *Live and Let Die* when Bolly first appeared. But it didn't come easy! When Albert Broccoli, producer of 007 first asked Bollinger to use their champagnes, Bollinger turned them down! It wasn't until Broccoli and the then President of Bollinger, Christian Bizot, became friends that the collaboration started. In a simple gentleman's agreement, millions of pounds' worth of advertising was agreed with a handshake and a couple of free bottles. The good ol' way! A far cry from Heineken's recent £64 million deal for the *Spectre* advertising campaign.

I like wines which polarize people: there's too much beige in the world today as people try and cater for every taste. Like legendary Lilly Bollinger herself, Bolly's wines aren't scared about stepping on toes or upsetting anyone in the quest for quality. Bollinger was already a well-established House, but it wasn't until Madame Lilly Bollinger took up the reins in 1941 that it realized its full potential. Elizabeth Bollinger was born with Scottish blood. She was kind, incredibly spirited and ferociously entrepreneurial. Aged 42, she lost her husband in the Second World War and took control of the family firm with passion, vision and heart. At the time it was very unusual to have a woman in such a high position. Her leadership propelled Bollinger and champagne forever on a huge trajectory of success, and her no-nonsense approach is still felt at the House today.

Bollinger is the only house in the whole of the Champagne region to have its own cooper, a skilled craftsman whose sole purpose is to make and re-work oak barrels. I've seen the results of his work: cellars containing 3,500 polished, grained oak barrels which smell incredible, woody, sweet and perfumed.

Bollinger's French oak barrels are never made from new oak but are bought from their sister estate Chanson, a top quality Burgundy producer. Using used or older oak barrels means the flavour imparted by the wood is very subtle, as some of the oak barrels are over 100 years old. Every single bottle of Bollinger has oaked wine components in the blend, a 100% for the top Grande Année expressions. The use of oak impacts two things on the wine, light oxidation and texture, which translates to richness and golden flavour in the finished champagnes. Their extended ageing in these barrels of every single bottle means the wines are softer in style and rounder in texture when they are finally released. Bollinger alongside Krug and Billecart Salmon are the gatekeepers of this rich, oaked style of Champers. Both feature in this book, no prizes for guessing I like this style.

Under Bollinger's winery is a labyrinth of 6 km of cellars. Resting peacefully in the dark, and rather scary cellars are 12 million bottles of reserve champagne. This is really what sets Bollinger apart: they only release 3 million bottles a year, showing that for Bollinger nothing gets in the way of quality. These 12 million bottles are resting quietly on cork and could be released as champagne in their own right, but Kauffmann, the Chef du Cave at Bollinger, keeps the bottles and ages them carefully to blend back into the champagnes he does release. All champagne houses keep reserve wines, but no other major house goes to the extra work and expense in keeping the reserve wine under cork, and is essentially ageing the champagne twice. This adds a unique complexity and toasty richness to the wines, just as double-cooked chips are even more delicious than their single counterparts.

Bollinger's house style is powerful, rich and stylish, appealing to discerning and new champagne lovers. For a house with such market presence in supermarkets and high street restaurants, Bollinger's quality and brand is in a league of its own, the best of the best. What better champagne to represent Queen and Country?

Bollinger
Special Cuvée

Tasting notes: Russet apple and dried figs, pine kernels, toffee apples and beeswax lead into floral highlights, chamomile and tea. Bags of crunchy red apples and pecan pie with cream.

Bollinger's flagship, and with good reason. Few Brut NVs are as rich and delicious as Bollinger's Special Cuvée. Note, the name is Special which of course is an English word rather than French which goes to show the House's affinity and ties with the UK. The name was given to the House Brut in 1911 when Georges Bollinger, head of the House at the time knocked heads with his UK importer Mentzendorff (who still represent the House today) and the name was born. Pinot dominant, with a splash of Chardonnay and a seasoning of Meunier this benchmark style is a blend of over 240 different components from Premier and Grand Cru vineyards. Partial vinification in oak casks, together with the use of Bollinger's secret weapon; the reserve wines mean that this truly is a tour de force in the Brut NV arena, and stands up against many other houses' top cuvées. Like Lilly, I could drink this every day!

TYPE Multi-Vintage Brut

STYLE Glorious, golden richness

PRICE 🍾🍾

STOCKISTS High street

TOAST 🍞🍞🍞

FOOD Roasted pork loin with pancetta, apples and figs

OCCASION *Skyfall is on telly*

Bollinger
La Grande Année 2007

Tasting notes: Brioche with raisins and candied fruit flavours foam together with crème patisserie. Bright fresh fruits, red apples and orange peel play on the palate with lemon curd on buttered toast. Complex rich and round, mega!

Seems very fitting that James Bond's favourite fizz arrived in (2)007! This is Bollinger's celebration of a singular year, that sourced 91% Grand Cru vineyards. Pinot dominant naturally with 70% of fruit from Ay, the hills behind the House and Verzenay. The Chardonnay proportion is from the Côte des Blancs; Avize, Chouilly and Le Mesnil which keep this wine incredibly sapid and fresh. 2007 was a varied year in Champagne, and didn't suit every producer as many picked their grapes too early. Bollinger nailed it, and this 2007 expression is classically round and vinous (wine-like) with a confident freshness. 100% aged in small oak barrels, then eight years resting quietly under Lilly's House on lees mean this champagne is ready to pop now, or can be cellared until 2025 no problem. This really is one of the best value prestige cuvées there is.

TYPE Prestige Cuvée, Vintage Brut

STYLE The ultimate gratification

PRICE 🄔🄔🄔

STOCKISTS High street

TOAST 🏠🏠🏠🏠

FOOD Butter roasted pork chops with parsnips and orange, or injera with masala chickpeas

OCCASION Hogmanay

Clos Cazals vines, Mesnil-sur-Oger

Clos Cazals

champagne-claude-cazals.net

Founded in 1897, Champagne Cazals has a long history of winemaking, but has only recently started to unlock its quality potential. Delphine Cazals is now taking the family business forward and is making some radical changes in her home town of Oger, down in the Côte des Blancs. The winery is based three minutes' drive away from her family home in Le Mesnil-sur-Oger, next door to the famous champagne House of Salon. The Cazals are sitting on a gold mine of potential for their own champagnes, still undiscovered by most. However, the family are already well known in the region as Delphine's father invented the gyropallate, which changed the face of all champagne production. This machine is a mechanized way of riddling champagne bottles in the cellar, which is now adopted in every single champagne house and traditional sparkling wine producer in the world.

Riddling sounds like something Rumpelstiltskin would do, but it is in fact a quintessential part of making champagne. All champagnes undergo a long period of ageing, as the second fermentation takes place. Riddling is essentially turning the champagne bottles in the cellar, by a few degrees, over a few years to move the lees, which are the dead yeast sediments left after the fermentation, very slowly into the neck of the bottle before disgorgement. This process was invented by Veuve Clicquot and is the removal of the lees, which after riddling are deposited in the very top of the bottle.

Cazals have some of the best vineyards in the whole of the region, and only now are realizing their potential as historically they sold most of their production to Bollinger and Moët for their top cuvées. Delphine Cazals is the envy of every single champagne house in the region, as she has the only 'Clos' or single, walled vineyard in the town of Oger. Together with the neighbouring town of Le Mesnil, Oger produces 100% Grand Cru wine, the best Chardonnay in the whole region due to the high chalk content and Kimmeridgian soils — this simply translates into the best wines of the area.

Cazals have some of the best vineyards in the whole of the region, and only now are realizing their potential

Single vineyard champagne is always unique, as historically champagne is always a blended wine from different vineyards and areas. Clos wines are very rare, expensive and special as they are only made in very small quantities; Cazals only produce a few thousand bottles, and are a true expression of the terroir. Krug, who produce a single vineyard three minutes' drive away in Le Mesnil sell their Clos du Mesnil for £400 a bottle. Delphine sells hers for £70.

Clos Cazals
Millésime 2008

Tasting notes: This champagne is bursting with deliciousness. Aromas of buttery lemon curd on toast strewn with Starburst fruits. White flowers and peaches lead into top-end toastiness with flavours of oatcakes and croissants. The fizz is rounded and foaming with a zappy chalky character which adds complexity and length to the palate, typical of top level Chardonnay from this area.

Sourced exclusively from Delphine's Grand Cru vineyards, she usually sells these grapes to other houses for their Prestige Cuvées. However, the 2008 vintages were so good she decided to bottle it herself! She then aged it in the cellars under her Mum's house on lees for an extended seven years before disgorgement, longer than many top champagnes from more famous houses. This has enabled the style to develop incredible richness and toastiness in flavour, and a softness across the palate. This is pure expression of Delphine's prime situated vines on the Côte des Blancs, a singular expression of the Chardonnay grape, paired with the epicness of the 2008 vintage means you are getting a taste of a £100+ champagne, for closer to £30. Quality of this value doesn't come round very often, so make sure you snap some up!

TYPE Vintage Brut, Blanc de Blancs

STYLE Lemon Curd on Toast

PRICE 🅛🅛🅛

STOCKISTS Specialist

TOAST 🥂🥂🥂

FOOD Dominos Meat Feast with garlic dip

OCCASION Thirsty Thursday, or a semi-important anniversary

Clos Cazals
Blanc de Blancs 2005

Tasting notes: Perfumed and ripe nose of bananas, pineapple and fruit. Perfume of white flowers, jasmine and white peach lead into shortbread, buttered toasted white Hovis. There is a sapid and saline chalky character which adds freshness, depth and deliciousness across the foaming, golden palate.

Planted in the 1950s by her father and grandfather, this special walled vineyard sits under a small church and the steep slopes of the Côte des Blancs. These old vines produce wines with amazing flavour and concentration which translates into the purity and intensity of the Clos Cazals Champagne. La Grande Dame, Veuve Clicquot original vineyards are ten meters away over the wall from the Clos, Cazals are in good company. The reason this Clos Champagne isn't world famous, or the Clos isn't a tourist destination is because Delphine keeps it private as her mum still lives there. The Clos is her back garden, and she doesn't want the hassle!

TYPE Prestige Cuvée, Vintage Extra Brut, Blanc de Blancs

STYLE Golden Granny Smith

PRICE £ £ £

STOCKISTS Specialist

TOAST 🍞🍞🍞

FOOD Flambé king prawns

OCCASION Christening of your first god child

Steps leading down to Charles Heidsieck's cellars

Charles Heidsieck's cellars date back to Roman times

Charles Heidsieck

charlesheidsieck.com

On my last visit to Champagne, I quizzed every Chef du Cave I met about what they drink when they're at home, a good gauge of quality and value I thought. Everyone gave me the same answer - apart from their own champagne and Gosset, they drink one house above all other: Charles Heidsieck. This is quite the accolade in itself, but if you dig a little deeper you find that this House deserves all the domestic respect it has and the reason it makes the most awarded champagnes in the world.

Charles Camille Heidsieck, was the nephew of the founder of the famous House Maison Heidsieck & Cie, and was a man about town. Although his flair, boisterous personality and salesmanship were an asset to the family firm, he was his own master and didn't enjoy the constraints of working under anyone. If Charles was around now, it's likely he would fit into the hipster scene of London Fields or Leith, with his silk cravats, waxed moustache and dandy dress sense. In 1851 at the ripe age of 29 he founded his own house, Champagne Charles Heidsieck, with the aim of creating a champagne which reflected his personality: stylish, fun and way over the top.

Picture the scene; a modern French gent travelling around Europe and as far as Russia, selling his champagnes and culture of post-revolutionary France. Charles was the talk of the town wherever he pitched up and the rich, famous and aristocracy all wanted a piece.

It wasn't until Charles went to America that he became a household name as 'Champagne Charlie'. The slick talking linguist was one of the first men to conquer the American market and he unapologetically sold himself to the States, as well as his prize-winning champagnes. Charles had the foresight to take full advantage of the American Dream, he became an overnight phenomenon shooting to celebrity status as young moneyed Americans bought into his story, his wines and his portrayal of the champagne lifestyle. At his height of fame, drinkers in bars were as likely to ask for a bottle of Charles, as they were a bottle of champagne.

Charles Heidsieck was arguably the first modern ambassador of the aspirational lifestyle which champagne now commands. His fame opened doors in the US and his network of influence grew to the top of the class ladder, as he was said to even clink coupes with Abraham Lincoln.

These relationships brought Charles good fortune, not only because he had devoted Charles fans on both sides of the pond which had a positive halo effect on his wine sales, but also for his own welfare. At the beginning of the American Civil War, Charles found himself in the wrong place at the wrong time, was captured and incarcerated in a Mississippi swamp jail! Not a place for a fine French dandy, he wrote home explaining he had to fight off crocodiles with bricks when the river flooded! Luckily for Charles, President Lincoln had Charles released and sent back to Champagne in one piece.

Since Charles's death in 1893, he has been personified in songs, films (Champagne Charlie starring none other than Hugh Grant-terrible film BTW) and books as the original ambassador for the glamour and adventure of the champagne lifestyle, encapsulating the essence of champagne and without the traditional formality. Cheers to Charles!

However Charles Heidsieck champagne wouldn't still have its reputation if it wasn't for the consistent and exceptional quality it showcases in every single bottle. Under the careful mastery of legendary Chef du Cave Thierry Roset who died in 2014, the same year he won the 'Winemaker of the Year' award at the highly acclaimed international Wine Challenge, the equivalent of the wine trade Oscars. Roset's wines have won more awards, medals and accolades than any other wine on the planet. The new Chef du Cave has big boots to fill, but they have the right man for the job, equally dapper and keen skier Cyril Brun, previously of Veuve Clicquot, is at the helm. He respects the continuity of style of Thierry and the passion and liveliness of Charles himself. Cyril, who makes his wines in an 'unapologetically rich style,' says, 'you can't take it too seriously' a refreshing change from other Grande Marques' formality.

What helps set Charles's apart is their rare declaration of vintage champagnes

The squatter bottles, with a thin neck, not only look smart but mean the champagne in the bottle ages more slowly, like it would if it was a magnum bottle, due to the smaller ratio between cork, air contact and wine. Charles is style in the glass, full, rich and very stylish. I love it.

What helps set Charles apart is their rare declaration of vintage champagnes, this means that the best vintages, i.e. the best quality wines, are held back as reserve wines and aged perfectly in the labyrinth of chalk cellars which tunnel eight km under the historic Champagne capital of Reims. This means the blended wines are more complex, more interesting and altogether more delicious than many champagnes out there. If I had the funds, I'd have a Charles tap in my kitchen and would drink it by the pint.

Charles Heidsieck
Brut Réserve

Tasting notes: Sunshine on the nose with dried stone fruits mingled with golden apple and Amalfi lemons. The palate is rich, foaming and full with Christmas cake spices and freshly baked butter biscuits.

The Brut Réserve NV is the entry point to the Charles range but by no means is an entry level champagne. It is arguably better quality than many Vintage champagnes. This is due to two reasons, the quality and flavour of the older reserve wines which make up almost half of the blend. The extended time ageing in the chalk cellars gives the wines more of a rich and polished style. This wine is the Chef du Cave's choice, not only because it is bloody delicious, but also because of their respect for the craftsmanship. To make these wines it involves a highly technical and frightfully complicated process of fractional blending of older reserve wines and younger blends, whilst maintaining the consistent pizzazz of the house style is impossibly difficult. The wines of Charles Heidsieck deserve the respect they have. Cyril told me himself that this wine was 'very dangerous' as it goes down the hatch a little too smoothly.

TYPE Multi-Vintage Brut

STYLE Complexity meets dangerous drinkability

PRICE 🍾🍾🍾

STOCKISTS High street

TOAST 🥂🥂🥂

FOOD Lobster bisque, or squid stuffed with boudin noir

OCCASION New Year's Day

Brut Réserve is multi-vintage champagne, worthy of a Prestige Cuvée. There is an equal split of each of the three main champagne grapes and in every bottle, 40% of the blend is older reserve wines, ten years old on average but many components dating back to the 1980s, meaning their Brut Réserve has wines over 30 years old! For me, this frankly is the best bang for buck Brut champagne you'll find. Maybe because I'm an 80s kid, but this champagne rattles me like few others.

Charles Heidsieck
Rosé Réserve

Tasting notes: Strawberry jam and peach orgy on a bed of gingerbread, sweet with cinnamon. The mouth is creamy, smooth and foaming with some blood orange, sweet savoury spices and ending with caramelized apple, tied up by tuck shop bootlaces.

Like most of Charles' range the rosé contains Chardonnay, Pinot Noir and Pinot Meunier in roughly equal parts with the addition of 5% red wine. This gives this wine a beautiful savoury character. The wines are sourced from some prime time sites; like Grand Cru Ambonnay, Ay and Riceys, an area in the south of the region famous for the richness of their Pinots. The base wine is predominantly the 2008 vintage, an epic year with the signature additional of older, complex reserve wines from Charles' secret stash. Aged for three years in the cellar, this pink beauty is ready to pop, and bloody delicious.

TYPE Multi-Vintage Rosé

STYLE Gingerbread man runs off with a Bakewell tart

PRICE £££

STOCKISTS High street

TOAST 🍞🍞

FOOD Strawberry soufflé with pistachio cream

OCCASION Netflix and chill

Charles Heidsieck
Blanc des Millenaires 1995

Tasting notes: Amazing, loaded with flavour and so lip-smackingly delicious you have to stop everything else you are doing just to appreciate the complexity and sheer enjoyment of flavour. Creamy, honeyed and all butter shortbread give way to lemon curd, toffee apple and razor minerality with waves of enveloping pleasure.

A vision of the Côte des Blancs sourced from the four titan villages of Cramant, Avize, Oger and Mesnil all top of the charts for Chardonnay. This monolithic style is anything but one-dimensional and showcases the very best of champagne Chardonnay, and the signature voluptuousness, fun and complexity of Charles Heidsieck.

After spending 17 years on lees in the 2000-year-old chalk cellars after which this wine is named, it was disgorged in 2014 and is drinking so well now. This champagne is brilliant. DO NOT serve too chilled. The next release of Blanc des Millenaires is set to be a much younger vintage, so definitely worth picking up a bottle of 1995, if you can find one.

TYPE Prestige Cuvée, Vintage Brut, Blanc de Blancs

STYLE Liquid, fizzy ecstasy

PRICE 🍾🍾🍾🍾

STOCKISTS Specialist

TOAST 🥂🥂🥂🥂🥂

FOOD Festive fare

OCCASION Christmas, and serve your in-laws Cava, this ain't for sharing

Delamotte

salondelamotte.com

There are few wines in Champagne which carry as many kudos, first rate reputation, genuine history and breathtaking quality. One such is Delamotte, older brother of the more mythical Champagne Salon. Both houses are located in the sleepy but iconic town of Le Mesnil-sur-Oger. Iconic because of Delamotte and Salon! This is the most prized, and priced, Grand Cru village in the Côte des Blancs, where Chardonnay thrives on the ancient chalk rich soils.

Champagne's fifth oldest House was founded in 1760 by François Delamotte, and was passed through the family until the Champagne royalty, Nonancourt family (owners of Laurent Perrier), took over the reins. LP then took over the running of both Delamotte and Champagne Salon in the 1980s and is now in charge of keeping these two iconic champagnes individual and true to their roots. Delamotte is essentially the second champagne of Salon, as they both share the same source of vines. This means, when Salon do not declare a vintage, whether the vintage was 100% optimum or not in the desirable Salon style, Delamotte gets all the declassified Salon fruit. The quality is cascaded down, straight into the steel tanks for Delamotte which is exactly what happened in the 2007 vintage. So enjoy a taste of Salon, but for a fraction of the price.

Delamotte
Champagne Delamotte 2007

Tasting notes: Scented with jasmine and orange flavour blossom, this is a tantalising wine: subtle and delicate with its fine, soft mousse. The wine is persistent and satisfying as it deepens in the mouth, hinting at richness and complexity to come.

Delamotte, like Salon, is an advocate of Chardonnay. All the grapes for this Blanc de Blancs is sourced from 100% Grand Cru vineyards of the chalky slopes of the Côte des Blancs. 2007 was a good year, and after eight years of careful ageing and maturation the Delamotte Blanc de Blancs is ripe and open now, or will cellar and develop beautifully for the next 10 to 15 years... if you can wait that long!

TYPE Vintage Brut, Blanc de Blancs

STYLE Wine's golden fleece

PRICE 💷💷💷

STOCKISTS Specialist

TOAST 🥂🥂🥂

FOOD Turkey sandwiches

OCCASION Bracing walk on Boxing Day

Cave etching in the Veuve Clicquot cellars

Chalk cellars at Deutz

Deutz

champagne-deutz.com

Deutz is a champagne House which has forged its reputation on quality and discretion. Established by Germans William Deutz and Pierre Geldermann in 1828 in the town of Ay (throwing distance from Bolly), it remains one of the unsung Grande Marques, as the quality of their range rivals any of their contemporaries.

The Deutz family lived at the historic and beautiful house, adjacent to the winery until the 1980s when the company was sold to Louis Roederer. The family would only agree to sell to a company who understood their quest for quality, and no ones knows integrity like Roederer.

There has been a huge amount of investment into the winery since then, at least €20 million! Although production has expanded which can mean a drop in quality but the hallmark of pleasure to price has been maintained. France is their biggest market by a long way, which is always an important gauge: the French have a longer relationship with champagne than with anyone else. They are an understated house considering their long history and legacy of pure, elegant champagne styles. I was super impressed with their entire range, and with increased production at the house, expect to see more and more of champagne Deutz on the shelves and on Wine Lists.

Deutz
Brut Classic

Tasting notes: Smooth and friendly, it showcases fresh white flowers, sweet gorse on the nose. Palate is supple, round and dangerously smooth with toasted almonds, citrus and stone fruit style finishing with golden orchard fruit which tantalizes the taste buds with flirtatious subtlety.

True essence of elegance and subtly, the Deutz signature. An equal blend of Chardonnay, Pinot Noir and Pinot Meunier from Grand and Premier Cru vineyards from all over the Champagne region from Deutz's large network of contract grape growers who cover a whopping 245 hectares of vineyards. This harmonic style has up to 40% reserve wine blended in for complexity and depth of flavour, but unlike Charles who use a similar amount, the wines are restrained rather than showy. Further ageing for three years in Deutz 'Berceau', or cots where they rest their infant bottles in the deep chalk cellars, and only release when they have reached their prime.

TYPE Multi-Vintage Brut

STYLE Class in a glass

PRICE £ £

STOCKISTS High street

TOAST 🍞🍞

FOOD Salmon steaks and colourful salads

OCCASION Summer thirst quencher

Deutz
Rosé

Tasting notes: Pretty pink colour, appealing nose of floral rosé sweetness and fragrant raspberry fruits. The palate is elegant and bright with puckering pomegranate and red current flavours. Romantic style, flows silkily over the palate, rounded fizz with a toasted strawberry meringue finish.

This Pinot dominant champagne has been mixed with 20% Chardonnay for freshness and structure, 8% of the Pinot is made as a red wine and blended into the finished base wine for colour and flavour. The red Pinot component comes from the hills behind the winery which boast some of the best Pinot Noir in the whole region; Ay and Mareuil-sur-Ay. Aged for three years in 'Berceau' before release, this rosé is one of best bang for buck surprises of my recent tastings, I couldn't recommend it more.

TYPE Multi-Vintage Rosé

STYLE Strawberries and cream

PRICE ££

STOCKISTS High street

TOAST

FOOD Thai fish cakes or duck with cranberries

OCCASION Your best friend's wedding

Didier Chopin

champagne-chopin-didier.com

Chardonnay and Pinot Noir make some of the best, most expensive wine in the world, and are planted all around the globe. This noble duo are also widely identifiable and a quality reference to customers. Pinot Meunier completes the holy trinity of champagne grapes, it is less well travelled and often considered the ugly cousin. But it's not all bad: it should count itself lucky, as there are actually six grape varieties allowed in Champagne. The forgotten siblings are Pinot Blanc, Petit Meslier and Arbane which are planted in teeny tiny quantities. But the threesome in the limelight are at the forefront of quality, and commercial champagne styles.

There is a renaissance for Meunier and not only because it makes up large proportions of two of the world's most sought after and awarded champagnes; Krug and Charles Heidsieck. But because of the styles its creates, it gives 'more' sooner to champagnes. It doesn't need ten years in the cellar to develop flavour and richness, or require manipulation in the same way its nobler siblings often need. It creates easier, fruity and refreshing

wine styles, and thrives in those vineyards where Chardonnay and Pinot cannot. Many champagne houses have been dismissive of using the grape, because it is the cheapest grape in the market and it doesn't mature as well as its Chardonnay or Pinot Noir. It has also been a way to differentiate themselves from other champagne producers, who do use the grape within the blends.

It's all about to change. The Didier Chopin Brut is an indicator that Meunier can create lovely styles at very affordable prices, as well as top end cuvées. This small-scale operation in the Vallée de la Marne is run by Didier, his wife Karine and their two children. They create drinkable, go-to styles when you are just gasping for a glass of the good stuff.

Didier Chopin
Brut

Tasting notes: Fruity, toasty Blanc de Noirs style champagne. Red apple, ripe stone fruit, brioche and floral aromas, fuller bodied than many Chardonnay dominant styles with sweet and softly foaming mousse.

A blend of Pinot Meunier and Pinot Noir, this Blanc de Noirs style is ripe and full-bodied. Aged on lees for three years before release mean Didier's champagne has fruit weight and glorious biscuit intensity, and you don't need to break the bank.

TYPE Multi-Vintage Brut, Blanc de Noirs

STYLE Ripe, honeyed freshness

PRICE 🍾🍾

STOCKISTS Specialist

TOAST 🍞🍞🍞

FOOD Chicken nuggets, or sandy sarnies on the beach

OCCASION First hint of summer

Moët & Chandon vineyards on the Côte des Blancs

Dom Perignon

domperignon.com

Dom, what else?

The myth, the legend. The most premium champagne on the market, and yes, believe the hype. Dom Perignon is the Prestige Cuvée of Moët & Chandon, the largest champagne producer in the world, and part of the goliath luxury brand owner LVMH which includes Dior, Chanel, Louis Vuitton, Champagne Ruinart, Veuve Clicquot and many others under its chic umbrella. Out of all luxury brands of champagne, Dom is universally the coolest, the most famous, the most widely available and with good reason: it's bloody delicious.

My first taste of Dom was when I was 17. My twin brother threw a surprise party for me and a few friends before we moved to France for our first snowboard season. We were fresh out of catering school and my friend Pete had appropriated a bottle of 1996 from his work. We shot the cork into the street in fits of giggles, but the laughter stopped as soon as I wet my whistle. I didn't know wine or champagne could taste like that, and it had a lasting effect on me.

11 years later, I am sitting in the private tasting room of Hautvillers Abbey, sleet lashing against the window of the spiritual cradle of champagne, and the resting place of Dom Perignon himself. I am sat with the man who is sculpting the destiny of Dom Perignon, Richard Geoffroy, the Chef du Cave, and the pure essence of the brand himself. We sit, taste, talk and discuss Dom Perignon and the story of Champagne over the vintages, ending with the recently disgorged P3 1973. Life goal achieved! I forgot to mention my first Dom Perignon experience.

Champagne is a weird wine as it is white wine made from red grapes

Champagne Dom Perignon has not been made ever since the eponymous monk was making wine in the late 1600s. It was created for the UK market in 1935 by owners Moët & Chandon, who sold 300 bottles of the 1921 vintage to their best private customers, this was over 200 years since the death of the acclaimed monk.

They needed a label and used the shield emblem from the label archives from the Moët & Chandon family, who actually lived at the Hautvillers Abbey until they were kicked out of their family home by the Germans during the war. What better name to give the original Prestige

Cuvée, than in homage to the godfather of champagne, the monk Dom Pierre Perignon? Only ever produced in years of exceptional quality, there have been only 42 vintages declared releases since the first 1921. Very rare to have two vintages declared in a row, even rarer three with 2004, 2005 and recent 2006 released back to back. But I expect there are increasing market pressures within a company the size of LVMH.

Regardless of fact and fiction surrounding the inventor of bubbles, Dom Perignon was hired by the Abbey of Hautvillers to produce wine, for which he had huge talent. Many of the champagne-making laws nowadays are still based on the original developments the monk made in the winery and the vineyards in the late 1600s. Dom Perignon was enterprising, and a great winemaker and was appointed by the church to run and turn a profit at the large Abbey of Hautvillers. The Abbey controlled a large land holding in the area. Above his commercial responsibilities, he was a man of the cloth and wished to create the most heavenly wine he could. This drove Dom in search of perfection through divinity.

As Dom Pierre's work began to take effect, the quality of the still wines of Hautvillers became the talk of the town,

and it wasn't long before news of the great wines floated down the Marne river to Paris and were soon to be snapped up by the Royal Courts. Even though at this time it was long before Hautvillers was famous for bubbles. This had an important halo effect on the Abbey's wines, for as soon as Royal lips endorsed the wines of the Abbey, every man and his dog wanted them all across Europe.

It was created for the UK market in 1935 by owners Moët & Chandon, who sold 300 bottles of the 1921 vintage to their best private customers

The Abbey taxed the local residents, and took payment in an agricultural currency, grapes. Dom was the one to vinify the grapes coming into the Abbey from all the different local farms and blend them together, giving him a view of the different quality levels from the different areas. This gave the monk an understanding of the vital aspect in the champagne-making process: blending different wines together to improve quality. This was a revolutionary step forward.

Champagne is a weird wine as it is white wine made from red grapes. All grape juice is clear, and any colour in red or rosé wine is attained by the skins; the longer you leave the juice in contact with the skins, the deeper colour of the red.

All champagne in the 1600s was a rusty pink colour, what they called 'oeil de perdrix' or the eye of the partridge, referring to the tawny eyes of the local bird. He was the first to challenge the pressing method to make wine – to start pressing the grapes gently, extracting the clear juice without taking any colour from the skins. This was a huge breakthrough and every champagne house will forever utilise and be grateful for this technique.

There has been no one true inventor of champagne, it is a human product. It has been constantly evolved and challenged and refined over the centuries. The people of Champagne have been brave enough to innovate, to develop, challenge and improve techniques and quality steadily over the years. But there has been no one individual so important to the overall quality as Dom Perignon, which is why many of the champagne houses I have visited, big or small, old or new, have an effigy of the monk sitting in pride of place in the winery.

Richard Geoffroy has been 'pushing the envelope' since 1990

Fast-forward 400 years or so and Hautvillers has another man in charge. Richard Geoffroy has been 'pushing the

envelope' since 1990 when he started work at Dom Perignon. Focused, disciplined and stylish, Richard oozes class and sophistication, and this has helped earn him the top seat in Champagne. He was born and raised Champenois, from a family of grape growers and still feels part of the wine growing community. A physician by training, he claims his medical background has given him both instinct and rationality, which helps him deal with his enormous responsibility. He rejects the comfort zone that many houses have built for themselves, creating consistent styles every year in a non-vintage champagne. He pushes to find potential in all aspect of production, the wine growers, the grapes, his winemakers and himself more than anyone else. The responsibility of blending one of the most famous wines on Earth, travelling the world endorsing his creation and declaration of Vintage Dom Perignon, whilst managing the politics of a major luxury goods conglomerate, must be a hectic schedule, but as Richard puts it, 'It's all about champagne'.

There has been no true inventor of champagne, it is a human product.

The production total of DP is as closely a guarded secret as the Holy Grail. I've heard anything from two to eight million bottles each release, but likely to be somewhere in the middle. Big production is often scoffed at in the wine trade, as large volume means diluted quality, but with DP this couldn't be further from the truth.

Considering owners Moët & Chandon

are the largest vineyard holders in the whole region and have access to more of the best vineyards than anyone else.

'It's all about champagne'

He explains that his job is a constant evolution; Dom Perignon is always pushing the boundaries and will never be in a settled state. Unlike many great champagnes, DP is a vintage wine, changing every year and is only made when the quality is right. Each release showcases the best of the vintage, whilst encapsulating the Dom Perignon style. No easy feat when you are blending thousands of individual components to achieve a final blend in a cohesive style.

Like the region of Champagne itself, tension and balance are vital in the style of Dom Perignon. The tension Richard builds into his wines is a tightrope walk between the Dom Perignon philosophy and the constraints of vintage which yield different wines and results every year. Paired with the duality of champagne's best quality grapes; Chardonnay and Pinot Noir which roughly feature 50/50 depending on the vintage. It is a yin and yang project he explains: the tension comes from the opposing and complementary relationships between these four factors. The fifth element, and just as important as the other four, is Richard himself.

He is passionate about vintage champagne, which contributes to only 6% of total champagne production, a lot of which I think must be Dom Perignon. He challenges why other houses don't champion more vintages, the norm in all other wine regions. His approach is all or nothing. 'Champagne is one of the great terroir on the wine planet, and Champenois need to represent the vintage of these great terroirs'. I'm inclined to believe him, but to be fair it's easier to say that when you have access to the best vineyards in the entire region.

Dom Perignon is now as famous as an object of luxury culture, as a quality champagne. The labels have been glamorized by the likes of Andy Warhol, David Lynch and Björk. The drinking of DP has been popularized by rap and pop cultures alike as the essence of desirability. Richard respects everyone who drinks it, even if they are spraying it on to strangers on the dance floor; this is still champagne, this glamour is as important a factor as anything else. He understands the population of DP drinkers is very diverse, and is happy if there is enough people drinking it with good reasons. They might have different good reasons, but they are enjoying champagne nonetheless.

Richard Geoffroy, is without a doubt one of the brilliant minds of champagne today. He knows no complacency. His approach seems more philosophical than tactile and he is on a mission to make the best wines he can which he does with great affect.

The Dom Perignon range is sheer class in a glass, each expressive of the vintage year and of the quintessential DP style. Like the monk Dom Perignon himself Richard is pushing the boundaries of what champagne is, and what his wines are. But unlike Dom, who was looking for divinity through his production, Richard only wants people to appreciate the wines and to enjoy them. I sure do, and next time you see a bottle of DP on the shelf, pick it up and join the brotherhood.

Dom Perignon
Vintage 2006

Tasting notes: Bright and luminous in the glass. Hallmark reductive in style, which translates into an almost smoky, Guy Fawkes Night aroma. Backed up with upfront candied fruits and salted caramels. Round in the palate, silkier than it is creamy with notes of toasted nuts, citrus, white peach, chalk and sweet saline with hints of licorice enveloping the ultimate finish.

2006 was the most challenging vintage in 25 years for Richard Geoffroy and team, and ultimately the most rewarding as he pushed the boat out even more than usual to create this special balance of Chardonnay, which makes up just over half of the blend, and Pinot Noir. Dom Perignon is always made from all 17 Grand Cru vineyards of champagne, including the Premier Cru vineyard in front of the Abbey at Hautvillers in homage to the man himself.

TYPE Prestige Cuvée, Vintage Brut

STYLE Expressive, ultimately stylish

PRICE 🅴🅴🅴🅴

STOCKISTS High street

TOAST 🍞🍞

FOOD Savoury crepes or Thai chicken

OCCASION Any worth celebrating

Dom Perignon
Rosé 2004

Tasting notes: Honestly, there are few rosés I've tasted in my life that really blew me away. This is one of them. Quintessential DP style; precise, polished and clean with the fruit, salinity, intensity and structure of a fine red, meeting over finely grained bubbles and freshness. This wine is a sheer joy, it's powerful! WOW!

This is a wine which is dedicated to Pinot Noir, using 28% percent of red grape which is unprecedented in champagne. This use of red wine means it is one-third of the structure of a red wine, combining all the best traits of champagne using one of the wine lover's favourite grapes: Pinot Noir.

TYPE Prestige Cuvée, Vintage Rosé

STYLE Complexity meets intensity

PRICE 💷💷💷💷💷

STOCKISTS Specialist

TOAST 🍞🍞

FOOD All the meals! This wine screams for blood… Duck breast with roasted mango or chocolate tart with stewed cranberries

OCCASION When you need to impress

Young vines close to Épernay

ASSAMY
(1868)

Graffiti in the cellars of Pol Roger, Épernay

Gosset

champagne-gosset.com

Gosset is Champagne's oldest winery, established in 1584. Ruinart is the oldest champagne House, but you can't make champagne without a winery and access to grapes, and Gosset has been fine tuning its wine for well over 400 years.

Family owned, Gosset is among the top quality players of champagne quality yet remain stoically in the background. When your wines are this good there is no need of big marketing budgets, this House allows its wines to do all the talking. Originally based in Ay, a stone's throw from Bollinger, it moved production and cellars up the road to beside Pol Roger in the epicentre of champagne, Épernay on Champagne's most prestigious address; Rue de Champagne. On my visits to Champagne, I always ask the Chefs du Cave what they like to drink at home, other than their own brand and Charles Heidsieck, Gosset was by far the most talked about.

With relatively small production, Gosset is a reflection of handcrafted artisanal champagne in the quest of unfaltering quality over quantity. Gosset's care and attention to create these styles means they can be paired with an array of foods and flavours.

When your wines are this good there is no need of big marketing budgets

Like a few of the most artisanal champagne producers, Gosset tend to avoid malolactic fermentation which means they can age magnificently well. These are true gastronomic champagnes and wouldn't be out of place on any of the top Michelin Star tables.

Gosset
Grande Réserve

Tasting notes: Dried fruits, apricots, figs and raisins fill the fragrance with sugar toasted nuts. The palate is super fresh, yet richly flavoured filled with bags of fruit and creamy almond croissant personality. Expressive style and very moreish.

This was Chef Michel Roux Jr's desert island wine on Radio 4's Desert Island Discs, and he has tasted a lot of incredible wine! My first introduction to Gosset was by the glass at Le Gavroche, and I always enjoyed steering customers towards this sophisticated champagne, richly textured, immediately enjoyable, and bloody brilliant with food. The Grande Réserve is the pure expression of Gosset, a blend of the three champagne grapes, the lion's share of Grand Cru Chardonnay. Based on the 2010 vintage with 25% reserve wine from the '08 and '09, with four years in the Gosset cellars before release, the result is a delicious toasty richness that retains the mineral signature of the House.

TYPE Multi-Vintage Brut

STYLE Flavoursome meets freshness

PRICE 🍷🍷🍷

STOCKISTS Specialist

TOAST 🍞🍞🍞

FOOD Foie gras and figs glazed with Madeira, or perfect with battered black pudding supper

OCCASION France beating England in the Six Nations

J.L. Vergnon

champagne-jl-vergnon.com

J.L. Vergnon is a tiny operation based in Mesnil-sur-Oger, run by the daring and talented Christophe Constant, a man who likes to push the boat out in the search of top quality.

The village is known for the quality of its Chardonnay which Christophe harnesses with expert skill into a range of diverse and utterly amazing champagnes. The grapes that Christophe uses are from vines planted in the 1960s, which give richly concentrated fruit, the maturity in the vines and grapes help him produce ambitious styles with great effect.

The winery is tiny for this boutique operation, but in this case great things come in small packages. Here they produce a mixture of forward-thinking champagnes with some old school techniques, such as a traditional champagne press which are mostly museum pieces nowadays. Christophe was one of the first in town to start using oak barrels for maturing and fermentation,

word travels fast in small towns and he was labelled as totally crazy by all his neighbours! But it did not take long for them to discover that his use of the barrels added body, flavour and texture to the wines. Most of the wines are zero or low dosage, and Christophe doesn't like to mask the vineyard expression with any additional sweetness.

Here they produce a mixture of forward thinking champagnes with some old school techniques

His appropriately named top wine is 'Confidence' which is 100% oak-fermented with no added sugar, for a tantalizingly fresh expression of Chardonnay and the Grand Cru vineyards of Le Mesnil.

J.L. Vergnon
Confidence Brut Nature 2009

Tasting notes: Elegant and supple fruit style, layered and complex. Exceptional freshness, paired with ripe apple and stone fruit character, the oak isn't obtrusive but fills the palate with fruit and gives a creamy richness and sweet spice. Sapid, mineral and fresh, this would appeal to Grand Cru Chablis drinkers. A grade.

All sourced from the old vines in Le Mesnil-sur-Oger and a little from neighbouring Oger, this bang tidy Champers is 100% vinified in Oak, half of which is brand new. A unique style combining vineyard expression, slight oxidation, and oak with a light touch in the winery means these champagnes are incredible now, but can be aged for 20 years. Really refreshing to see such experimentation and diversity in the icon town of Le Mesnil, as most producers play it safe down the middle of the road, but that ain't Christophe's style, and I think many people will follow suit. The 2009 was a great year and a very smart buy in Champagne, as the easier year of 2008 grabbed more headlines.

TYPE Vintage Brut Nature, Blanc de Blancs

STYLE Vibrant, expressive and sharp

PRICE 🍷🍷🍷

STOCKISTS Specialist

TOAST 🍞🍞🍞

FOOD Lobster with a gluttonous amount of béarnaise

OCCASION Sunday night on a bank holiday

Rather a lot of Pol Roger's Cuvée Sir Winston Churchill

Jacquesson

champagnejacquesson.com

The first time I met Jean-Hervé Chiquet, we had a bet – who could get to London first. I was getting the train back from Épernay–Paris–London that afternoon with a few minor waits at stations, while Jean-Hervé was driving from his home and winery in Dizy, Champagne to a hotel near Waterloo. I thought, surely the train is quicker than driving. Door to door, it took me six-and-a-half hours to get home that evening. Jean-Hervé did it in 5 hrs 45 mins. Jean-Hervé likes to take a risk, and true to form they pay off.

Jacquesson has gone through a lot of changes since it was established in 1798, but never as radical as when brothers Jean-Hervé and Laurent Chiquet took up the reins in 1988. Their father bought the champagne House in the late 1970s and the two brothers both saw the quality potential of the vineyards they had, and wanted to override the way Jacquesson Champagne was structured, grown, made and sold. Their father saw things very differently but after ten years of campaigning every morning, Dad finally gave in. Flash forward to 2000, and the brothers made yet further changes and overhauled their entire range of wines, feeling that the changes they had already made weren't reflected in the styles or quality of the wines.

Since these radical changes were introduced Jacquesson Champagne has dropped production by 40%, in the opposite direction of other successful champagne houses which would follow demand to produce more each year.

The discerning brothers only accept perfection, and whilst consistency isn't high on the agenda, quality and their vineyards dictate their production and wines. They produce a few single vineyard expressions each year, and one cuvée which they release twice, once when it's ready, and one later disgorgement release. This has simplified production, as opposed to making lots of various blends of lesser quality.

Jean-Hervé: 'Champagne is a wine; aromas are important. Bubbles are part of champagne, but not essential.'

> 'Champagne is a wine; aromas are important. Bubbles are part of champagne, but not essential.'

Jacquesson have pioneered a fresh philosophy to they way they make wines, producing only the best they can each year, regardless of what they did the year before. Creating wines which taste the same every year didn't seem right to them: to unlock quality why be pigeon-holed into uniformity? The wines they release change each year, but quality is foremost. This fresh approach is very rare in such a traditional, historic category like champagne and is totally commendable.

Since the brothers began their mission in 1988 they are now one of the most respected, prestigious and sought-after champagnes, and in the top five producers in the whole region for me. If you see a bottle of Jacquesson, buy it as the bottles are like gold dust.

Jacquesson
Cuvée no. 739

Tasting notes: Golden style with round, fleshy fruit on palate – white peach, pineapple and toasty apple crumble flavours with custard with a seasoning of funky spice. The mousse is soft and foamy with mineral zip, and sapid freshness. Vinified in oak, for a rounder, richer style.

Based on the 2011 vintage: 57% Chardonnay, 21% Pinot Noir, 22% Pinot Meunier with 31% Reserve wine, all vinified in oak, for a rounder, richer style.

The name of the Cuvée changes every year. It is a simple method to name a wine! 739 refers to a production number, opposed to a fanciful Cuveé name which the brothers started using in the year 2000. This is after they found an old cellar book, with Cuvée no.1 In 1898 which celebrated the 100th anniversary of the House. The next release will be 740. These wines age fantastically well, definitely worth holding on to a few bottles if you can.

TYPE Multi-Vintage Extra Brut

STYLE Expressive, candied-pineapple

PRICE 🪙🪙🪙

STOCKISTS Specialist

TOAST 🍞🍞

FOOD Smoked salmon rillettes with cucumber salsa

OCCASION Drinking alone, you won't want to share!

Jacquesson
Dizy Corne Bautray 2005

Tasting notes: Golden, bone dry and mineral the first impression of this wine is softly spoken. After some air, the single vineyard wine gives you an amazing taste of where it's grown. Mineral, chalky and fresh with white peach, almond milk and brioche climaxing in a zippy finish which goes on and on and on...

100% Chardonnay from their Dizy vineyard, this is one of the best Chardonnays in the Vallée de la Marne, an area more recognized for red wine production. This is a wine of the true Jacquesson expression of their single vineyards and Jean-Hervé explained they make great wines, opposed to just champagne. But as we now know, the Chiquet family like to go against the grain and Jean, 'Daddy Chiquet', planted Chardonnay in the 1960s. There is a link with all great wine in the world, and that is it comes from unique, exceptional terroir. The bubbles in champagne make up some of the charm of this wine, but it would be a great wine nonetheless. This single vineyard champagne is a true wine lover's dream, and it's very rare to taste such an expression of Chardonnay and Dizy terroir. This vineyard creates grapes which are so delicious, back in 2012 Jean-Hervé found that a wild boar had got into the vineyard and eaten 2000kg of their Chardonnay grapes, over a thousand bottles! If you are lucky enough to find a bottle of this very special wine, make sure the boars don't get to it first.

TYPE Vintage Extra Brut, Blanc de Blancs

STYLE French kissing Dizy Chardonnay

CHEF Jean-Hervé & Laurent Chiquet

PRICE 🍷🍷🍷🍷🍷

STOCKISTS Very specialist

TOAST 🍞🍞🍞

FOOD Pan roasted turbot, on the bone

OCCASION Very special

Krug

krug.com

"From the selection of grapes to the ageing of our cuvées in the cellars, patience and an understanding of time are fundamental values we respect. Krug won't be hurried. Time is one of our strengths."

— *Eric Lebel, Chef du Cave*

It doesn't get more special than Krug: the most expensive, stylish and most luxurious champagne House there is. And it is a well known aphrodisiac to boot! Krug is the undisputed King of champagne, all hail.

But considering the lofty mystique Krug now commands, the story started from humble beginnings. Joseph Krug, born in Mainz, Germany in the 1800s, was the man to change the face and style of champagne forever. After moving to France at the age of 24 with huge ambitions and a thirst for champagne, he started working as an accountant for the prominent Jacquesson Champagne.

After cutting his teeth and broadening his experience, he was not content with the variable, inconsistent style produced in each vintage from the champagne House, and left at the age of 42 to create a champagne which didn't yet exist: his own Champagne Krug.

The unknowns and variants in the weather mean that style and quality drastically alter from one year to the next. Joseph's philosophy was craftsmanship without compromise; his goal to produce the best champagne there had ever been, without the changeable restrictions of vintage variation. He wanted to create a cuvée which was the fullest expression of champagne, every year without fail. What he did revolutionized champagne for ever, and the Krug Champagne style is not only evident in bottles of Krug today, but in every House who produce non-vintage styles, many who can only endeavour to produce the magic that Krug does. Unlike the usual quality ladder of a champagne house from the cheapest NV to the most expensive Prestige Cuvée, Krug have no hierarchy, price or quality. This means all of what they produce is Prestige Cuvée quality.

Joseph's philosophy was craftsmanship without compromise; his goal to produce the best champagne there had ever been, without the changeable restrictions of vintage variation.

Krug's Non-Vintage champagne contains a spread of 15 different vintages, and with exceptional blending of individual components the style is consistent from each year's release to the next. With a higher proportion of older vintage wines in the blend, the wine style is richer, more flavoursome and more complex, benefiting from Krug's signature use of oak barrels. This means Krug's style is one of the richest expressions of champagne there is. Krug houses the most diverse palette of reserve wines in the whole of champagne with access to over 150 wines spanning 15 vintages.

With an obsession with detail and unfaltering patience, Olivier Krug (Joseph's great great grandson) creates wines which aren't only some of the best in the region, but some of the most prestigious.

Krug is expensive, but boy is it worth it.

The Clos du Mesnil vineyard, used to produce Krug's Clos du Mesnil

Krug
Grande Cuvée

Tasting notes: Absolute elegance and power. Deep gold, ripe and full with flavours of dried apricots, pineapple, marzipan and Christmas cake spices. The palate is intense and round with gingerbread, crème caramel, sugared almonds and buttered brioche.

Over 20 years are needed to create the Krug Grande Cuvée, and it is this patience and practice which means Krug champagne is one of the world's best champagnes. Detail is critical in the winery and the vineyards, where no grapes are used unless they are of best quality and famously use all three of champagne's grapes, including Pinot Meunier. The Grande Cuvée, although it is the 'entry' to the Krug range, gets the same respect as any of their single vineyards of vintage wines, which are some of the most expensive wines in the world. A complex blend of over 120 separate wines from 15 different vintages makes up the initial blend, which after careful combining is aged for a further six years in the cellar before release. Krug will cellar extremely well, and if you are lucky enough to afford it, it is well worth keeping a few bottles to pop on that special occasion.

TYPE Prestige Cuvée, Multi-Vintage Brut

STYLE Grand golden generosity

PRICE 🅔🅔🅔🅔

CHEF Eric Lebel

TOAST 🥂🥂🥂🥂

FOOD Hugely versatile due to its roundness and complexity

OCCASION Your sibling's wedding day breakfast with Eggs Benedict and black pudding – I did with my big bro!

The city of Reims is home to many of
the most famous champagne producers

Lanson

lansonchampagne.com

❧

Lanson are one of the largest champagne producers, and one of the most widely available. Established in 1760, it remains one of the oldest champagne Houses. It is based in the historic centre of Reims, where its 9 kms of cavernous chalk cellars run directly beneath the bustling streets of the town. These same cellars were used during the war as a makeshift village, deep enough to keep the population safe from the bombing above. There was a chapel at one end, carved into the soft chalk, there was a butcher and a temporary maternity ward for the four babies which were born down in the dark – even cattle were kept down there, if the walls could talk! Now it is a more subdued environment, better for the bubbly, where over 20 million bottles of Lanson Champagne sit quietly, waiting for their release.

'Maintaining freshness, power and fruit' is top of the agenda for Hervé Dantan, Chef du Cave and one of the most popular men in Champagne. He took on the responsibility of Lanson's five million bottle annual release from the legendary, late Jean-Paul Gandon who transformed Lanson champagnes over the last 40 years. Hervé is adding his own touch to the classic Lanson style, and making a few important changes in the winery which will slowly come to fruition over the next

few years. He has introduced more small tank selection, and particularly the use of large oak barrels for his reserve wines which give more diversity and complexity when he creates his famous blends. With Hervé at the helm, the wines will only get better and better.

Lanson's unique selling point is their use of non-malolactic fermentation, something which never translates very sexily to the final consumer. What this basically means is the conversation of acids in the wine: malic acids (think Granny Smith apples) to Lactic acids (think crème fraîche). When you don't do malolactic, you get a purer expression of the vineyards, and it keeps the wine fresher, leaner and greener. Neither technique is right or wrong, but non-malo styles are rarer, more discerning, less drinkable in youth but fantastic later. This is one of the many impressive signatures of Lanson Champagne: the wines do age very, very well.

Funnily enough, it wasn't until the 1960s that producers started doing malolactic fermentation due to improvements in technology and understanding of winemaking techniques. With a broad brush, you can say that malo styles of champagne can be drunk quicker, as they do not need as much ageing, which means customers enjoy the young champagnes more, and champagne houses can sell their stock quicker. But it's good to have diversity and hats off to Lanson for championing the 'original' style of champagne which is evident in every single bottle.

If you are looking for a classic champagne style, clean, fresh, vibrant and fruity, especially when on discount, Lanson Black Label is serious bang for buck. But for me, it was the top expressions of Lanson which got me excited.

'Maintaining freshness, power and fruit' is top of the agenda for Hervé Dantan, Chef du Cave and one of the most popular men in Champagne.

You will see Lanson widely distributed, heavily discounted in most supermarkets, corner shops and plastered over the TV when Wimbledon is on, but do not take this for a sign of lesser quality, quite the opposite. Lanson's Black Label, which is one of the most sold champagnes in the UK market, is a tour de force of quality. As Hervé told me, the NV is the most important wine to get right, as they sell more Black Label than any other of their wines.

Lanson
Noble Cuvée Blanc de Blancs 2000

Tasting notes: Sweet aromas of white flowers, hints of wild honey, spice and shortbread are both subtle but glorious. Flour, honeycomb and white peaches dance on the palate with soft, foaming sweetness, ending with the salinity and sapidity of Grand Cru Chardonnay.

Choice selection of the most elegant and finessed wines. This isn't a wine which is in your face or loud but an elegant expression of the best Chardonnay in Champagne, sourced from Avize and Cramant Grands Crus. With 14 years on lees, it has developed a richness, interest and quality which are rarely found on high street shelves. This is a connoisseur's choice.

TYPE Vintage Brut, Blanc de Blancs

STYLE Delightful celebration of Chardonnay

PRICE 🍷🍷🍷🍷

STOCKISTS High street, specialist

TOAST 🍞🍞🍞🍞

FOOD Aperitif, or white fish with beurre blanc

OCCASION You've quit your job to go surfing in Costa Rica

Lanson
Extra Age Brut

Tasting notes: Notes of biscuit, shortbread and almonds smash into lemon, spun sugar and ripe apples. Intense and long, with sweet citrus and almond notes – this is a champagne of incredible quality and value.

Created to celebrate 250 years of Lanson, the Extra Age is a combination of Lanson style, vineyard selection and modern chic. Extra Age is created only from Grand Cru vineyards from the 2003, 2004 and 2005 vintages, with ten years on lees minimum. This gives this wine all the time it needs to express the multi-layered complexity of this stunning multi-vintage blend of 60% Pinot Noir and 40% Chardonnay.

TYPE Multi-Vintage Brut

STYLE Lemon meringue pie

PRICE 🅛🅛🅛

STOCKISTS High street, supermarket

TOAST 🍞🍞🍞

FOOD Sourdough pizza with smoked mozzarella

OCCASION Toasting the start of the holidays

Laurent Perrier

laurent-perrier.com

I was lucky enough to have my induction to the Laurent Perrier House done by the celebrated and decisive Nicole Snozzi, its long standing ambassador. When I first met Nicole drinking Ultra Brut in central Reims, she barked at the young Sommelier in the bar as he took away the finished champagne bottle. She explained to me, turning your bottle upside down in an ice bucket is considered rude in Champagne, this was the tool used by prostitutes to empty guests' bottles quicker, and make them spend more money!

When you arrive at LP, the initial impact is the stately size of the place and beautifully manicured French gardens, as you would expect from the 4th largest champagne producer, who also own the iconic Delamotte and Salon champagnes. Nestled in front of the grand facade of Maison LP is a statue of a young boy peeing into a pond, with the words 'Ne Buvez Jamais d'Eau' transcribed beside him. This is LP; serious, sizable, impeccably turned out but also good fun.

Laurent Perrier's varied and fascinating story stretches back two hundred years, but it was the legendary Bernard de Nonancourt who was the Tour de Force behind LP's post-war success. He changed the face of this family champagne house after fighting courageously in the French Army and then the Resistance. He lost his dear brother Maurice, who would have been at the helm of the company if he had survived the war, to Nazi barbarism.

Bernard and his brother were young

Both were working away when a convoy of German trucks filled with armed soldiers arrived

men when the war broke out, still finishing their studies in Reims and had both begun an apprenticeship at Delamotte Champagne House in Le Mesnil-sur-Oger, arguably the best vineyard site in the entire Champagne region, the adjacent house of famous Salon. Both were working away when a convoy of German trucks filled with armed soldiers arrived at Salon's doors. With the order from Marshall Goering, who was responsible for keeping the German armies stocked with the finest champagnes, the Germans looted the Salon cellar, plundering every last bottle of the top 1928 vintage Blanc de Blancs.

Years later, on the 4th of May 1944, Bernard's tank regiment was the first on the scene to Hitler's Eagle's Nest following his suicide in his Berlin Bunker.

This was Nazi Germany's cave of wonders, as publicized by *The Monuments Men* directed by George Clooney, hoarding the paintings, sculptures, jewellery and wine plundered during the war. Being from Champagne, Bernard was ordered in first, and, once the dust had cleared from the dynamited armoured doors, he switched his torch on to find a true cave of wonders. Tens of thousands of the best wines in the world, the greatest wines of Bordeaux and Burgundy plundered over the previous years of occupation, the finest Cognacs of the last century, Mumm, Pommery and Lanson champagnes perfectly cellared in the dark, deep dungeon Hitler had created. It must have been a sight for sore eyes! But the wine they chose to toast the victory, the end of the war and their own success was Salon 1928, the exact same wine which Bernard and Maurice had seen plundered all those years before.

The war had a profound effect on Bernard de Nonancourt, especially following the death of his brother. Perhaps this gave Bernard the additional drive to supreme success, changing the fortunes of not just his champagne House, but all of champagne.

LP was also the first House to launch rosé en masse, which in 1968 made them the laughing stock of the fellow Champenois. LP are the ones laughing now, as their iconic Rosé Brut is the best selling champagne rosé in the world.

Under Bernard, Laurent Perrier launched the Grand Siècle, their Prestige Cuvée with its unique bottle shape based on an original bell-shaped champagne bottle which was found discarded in the grounds of Versailles, probably after one of Louis XV's extravagant parties. Alongside Krug, the Grand Siècle was the first top Prestige Cuvée from a champagne house to use multi-vintages to maintain quality

and style for each release. Up until then, top cuvées were only vintage specific, and only released in good and great years, but this method has paved the way for just about every other top producer to follow in Bernard's footsteps.

Fashions come and go with the seasons, but one of the newer trends out of champagne in recent years is the 'zero dosage' style. These are champagnes with no added sugar, bone dry, razor fresh; a pure tasting style of champagne perfect with oysters or sushi. LP again were the leaders of the pack, launching 'Grands Vins Sans Sucre' in the 1800s; now the Laurent Perrier Ultra Brut is the benchmark style of this category.

LP have recently been pioneers too, as their new Multi-Vintage Brut is being launched in 2017. La Cuvée replaces their flagship Brut, with a new and stylish label change, increased Grand Cru Chardonnay and extended bottle age of up to four years meaning the LP range has never been richer, more toasty or tasted better.

Across LP's ranges, Bernard's philosophy is still evident today in the wines' freshness and elegance. Again LP were pioneers in using steel tanks to make their wines, which almost every producer in champagne now does. Steel tanks keep the wines fresher, fruitier and create more elegant styles of champagne. Next time you pick up a bottle of Laurent Perrier, give a thought to the legendary figure, the war hero, and businessman who changed the way we all drink champagne. Cheers to Bernard!

Laurent Perrier
Grand Siècle

Tasting notes: Clean, intense and richly flavoured. The candied citrus and orchard fruits wash over the palate with shortbread, brioche and oatmeal character, both sapid and lip-puckeringly delicious. Mineral, almost salty on the finish which makes you want to drink it! Elegance, full of finesse and power, an exceptional expression of champagne. It was served by the glass in Le Gavroche and was Chef Michel's go-to at the end of a service, and he has great taste.

When GS was introduced, many other houses had only vintage champagnes as their Prestige Cuvée. Blending is what champagne is all about and Laurent Perrier wanted to do something extra, something special which combined the very best elements of their champagnes. Combining structure with finesse and elegance, Grand Siècle was born, keeping a consistent style year on year. Only ever made from 100% Grand Cru with a blend of approx 55% Chardonnay and 45% Pinot Noir for each release. It's always made with three vintages; the older vintages are always Chardonnay to keep freshness and complexity. This wine is a base of 2002, an incredible vintage in Champagne blended with 1999 and 1997. Few Prestige Cuvées are this complex, and utterly special.

TYPE Prestige Cuvée, Multi-Vintage Brut

STYLE The finest silk

PRICE 💷💷💷💷

STOCKISTS Specialist

TOAST 🥂🥂🥂

FOOD Dover sole, dripping in butter, shrimps and potato fondant

OCCASION Valentine's day

Laurent Perrier
Ultra Brut

Tasting notes: Green mango and melon skin give an immediate sweet fruit profile which moves away to a crystal-like edge of mineral and steely freshness which cuts across the palate like a razor slicing through an Amalfi lemon.

The original Ultra Brut, this is as sharp as an Opinel and as fresh as an Alpine spring! This low-sugar style is a blend of 12 different villages' wines across Champagne, chosen for their richer fruit style and balancing freshness.

TYPE Multi-Vintage Ultra Brut

STYLE Razor fresh

PRICE ●●●

STOCKISTS High street

TOAST 🍞🍞

FOOD Oysters, caviar and devilled eggs

OCCASION Pre-dinner aperitif, or post-dinner sharpener

Laurent Perrier
Rosé

Tasting notes: A glass of pink exuberance; cherry, strawberry, red fruit, those bootlace sweeties fill your taste buds, a richly textured palate thick with strawberries and clotted cream with a wash of cleansing lemony freshness. The finish is round and spicy, with a turn of cracked black pepper.

Before 1968, when LP launched their rosé, pink champagne wasn't a popular style. It was LP that championed the pink with this revolutionary multi-vintage rosé and so a whole category was born. This is 100% Pinot Noir sourced from a multitude of cru vineyards, many Grands Crus from Montaigne de Reims including the famous area of Bouzy, famed for its exceptional Pinot Noir. Macerated like a red wine to draw out colour, flavour and texture from the grape skins means that LP rosé has a rich style with bags of fruit, wine-like character, volume on the palate and champagne magic. Four years in LP cellars before release, this is a benchmark style of rosé champagne and one of the most popular.

TYPE Multi-Vintage Rosé

STYLE Rose petals and strawberries

PRICE ⓵ⓛⓛ

STOCKISTS High street

TOAST 🍞🍞

FOOD Seared tuna steaks with lime and chilli, steak tartare or homemade raspberry tarts

OCCASION Light the candles for a romantic night in

Charles Heidsieck cellars

Pol Roger cellars

Le Mesnil

champagnelemesnil.com

Le Mesnil Blanc de Blancs Grand Cru is made by the best co-operative wineries in the business, located in the heartland and Grand Cru area of Côte du Blancs, Le Mesnil-sur-Oger. A co-op winery works with grape growers who collectively manage the vines and the winery production. With 553 members, Le Mesnil co-op benefits from the quality of vineyards in the area, and the farmers benefit by the economies of scale, working with their neighbours to jointly make the best wines they can. The docile village of Mesnil is home to some of the titans of champagnes; Salon, Delamotte and the infamous Krug single vineyard expression, Clos du Mesnil, one the most expensive in the world. My first introduction to Le Mesnil champagnes was at Le Gavroche, as they used to make the 'House Champagne'. That business has now moved elsewhere, but Le Mesnil still produce their own label for Berry Brothers & Rudd of St James.

The co-op works with over 300 hectares of vines, half of which they own themselves and half they buy in from local farmers and growers, though only ever from Premier and Grand Cru vineyards. This access to the top vineyards in the Côte des Blanc is unprecedented, as the Chardonnay is the best in the region and is in huge demand from all the top producers. This means they either press the grapes on the Grande Marques' behalf, or sell wine in tank to truck up the road to the famous postcodes in Avize, Épernay and Reims. As the co-op has access to the top vineyards, it holds the keys to what they want and don't want to sell, and they keep the cream and sell the milk. The annual production is big, and their own bottled business is tiny in comparison at only 10% of annual production. The lion's share of their production they sell to the big and most famous names in Champagne for their own prestige.

All this means Le Mesnil Grand Cru Blanc de Blancs is one of the smartest buys you can make in all of champagne. The fruit they use is 100% Grand Cru, from the most famous Chardonnay town: Champagne. The co-op keeps all the best parcels for their own smaller bottled business, and sells what they need to the more famous producers, who take all the credit! Their own smaller bottled business is of exceptional value, as the champagne houses which buy wine from the co-op might retail their wines for five times the price! Gilles Marguet the talented and razor-sharp Director/Chef du Cave creates one of the best value Blanc de Blancs in all Champagne. This is worth searching for.

Le Mesnil
Grand Cru Blanc de Blancs

Tasting notes:White flowers, chamomile, citrus fruits and pain au raisin richness give volume and freshness across the palate. Oatcakes and lemon curd dance and play on the tongue, with a long fruit-filled and elegant finish.

Sourced from the chalkiest soils in the land from 100% Grand Cru vineyards, this force of Chardonnay is a blend of two different vintages; 2012, with a splash of 2011 reserve wine to add extra richness and depth of flavour on the palate. With over three years on lees this is a pure and racy style of Chardonnay which will drink well now, or age beautifully over the next 5-10 years.

TYPE Multi-Vintage Brut, Blanc de Blancs

STYLE Pure fruity elegance

PRICE 🌓🌓

STOCKISTS Specialist and posh supermarkets

TOAST 🍞🍞

FOOD Parma ham with chunks of Parmesan, or even fruit desserts

OCCASION Saturday

Louis Roederer

louis-roederer.com

Founded in 1776 and remains under family ownership. Louis Roederer Champagne is famous for many things, perhaps most for their prestige Cuvée Cristal, which has been endorsed by rap and hip hop culture for years, from P. Diddy to Jay Z. The House have now distanced themselves from such unwarranted sanctions from celebrities, after Frédéric Rouzaud CEO publicly asked rappers to stop spitting verse about Cristal! The quality of their wines is the only endorsement Roederer are interested in and they are titans of quality.

Louis Roederer are one of the pioneers of organics and biodynamics in Europe, let alone just the Champagne region.

I like a lot of champagne but, for me, Louis Roederer is the best quality, best value Grande Marque there is. Along with Bollinger, Roederer is the largest independent, family-owned and run champagne House in the region. The independent ownership means that although Roederer are big players in Champagne, it is still run like a boutique winery with no corporate obligation and their attention to detail is evident. At Lois Roederer they make fine wine first and bubbles second, but for the Chef du Cave, legendary Jean-Baptiste Lacaillon, expressing the sense of place is paramount. Unlike many of the larger Grande Marques it owns 240 prime time hectares of Premier and Grand Cru vineyards which supply the lion's share of the annual needs. This translates into total control of quality from the grapes in the vineyards, to the finished bubbles. Roederer has even deeper roots in the vineyards of champagne, started by the intuition of Louis Roederer himself who bought up a lot of vineyards when the price was low following the phylloxera epidemic in the late 1800s. Their vineyards are well situated across the three growing areas of champagne – Montagne de Reims, best situated for Pinot Noir; Vallée de la Marne, best for Pinot Meunier; and Côte des Blancs, one of the best Chardonnay terroirs in the world for its high content of chalk soils.

Louis Roederer are one of the pioneers of organics and biodynamics in Europe, let alone in just the Champagne region. Their intention is not to become a certified organic producer, but to constantly challenge techniques and improve quality, if quality wasn't improving they wouldn't do it. Jean-Baptiste's harvests are often 30% lower than his neighbours, but the increased class of each grape makes up for the smaller volume. At Roederer they take it another step back, and even have their own vine nursery to nurture the best clone selection from the very beginning. The attention to detail is immense; these champagnes are hand crafted and loved.

Each vineyard plot and parcel is kept separate until the blending or 'assemblage' takes place. This is no mean feat, as over 410 separate parcels and 450 tanks are used to create the famous styles that have earned Jean-Baptiste Lacaillon a sparkling reputation as one of the most respected and skilful winemakers in the world.

He is also a very lovely bloke. He explained to me that in blending there is a universal rule: if you add a weak wine to ten good wines, you make a bad wine. Only good wines make up the blends at Roederer. He describes himself as a conductor, blending the right music to create the Roederer universe and experience, and wants as much diversity as possible when combining and creating his blends. It's not a fixed recipe but a constant adaptation, and capturing the character of each vineyard's parcel is top priority at Roederer. For Jean-Baptiste his objective is to let his wines express his

wonderful terroirs, 'Chalk is the style of Roederer,' he explains.

Jean-Baptiste thrives for more expression of the terroir, and his grapes farmed biodynamically are healthier, tastier and make more expressive styles with more intensity. The more intensity and expression he finds in the vineyards, the better the wines are going to be. Now, 85% of all production is farmed organically, with the view to go 100% over the next ten years. Although this practice is best for quality, it is also very risky, as the use of sprays and agricultural chemicals in the vineyards protects the yields and more consistent supply each year.

In the winery, the same level of detail is maintained. Both steel and oak tanks are used extensively at Roederer. The large oak barrels Jean-Baptiste has introduced in his time there are both used for fermentation of young wines and for ageing his reserve wines. This clever, and delicate use of oak means the Roederer wine style has a softer, richer texture. The reserve wines used are all from single vineyards, which are up to ten years old, adding further complexity to his final wines. The iconic Brut Premier blend is made with up to 30% of these special, older reserve wines. This means he has a never-ending resource of complexity and flavour to add to his wines. When touring the cellar I noticed a few wine barrels beside the larger tanks of Reserve wines and JB explains that they are his climate change plan, as maybe one day they will need to make more still wine. The first time he was happy with the quality of the still was the 2015 vintage. So watch this space!

Cristal is a celebration of chalk

Louis Roederer is a titan of quality, a benchmark in style and creates some of the best Grande Marques Champagne there is. Their icon Cristal Prestige Cuvée has become famous as one of the top luxury products on Earth. Cristal is a celebration of chalk and quality and some of the best champagnes I have ever tasted. It remains a single estate wine, as it's been farmed from the same plots of vines for a long time. The wines' luxury and prestige associations are by no means a recent thing – it's long been a favourite of the rich and famous. Like Veuve Clicquot, Roederer champagnes were one of the first champagnes to enter the Russian market, and the royal family soon developed a liking of the Roederer style. So much so in fact that in 1876 Tsar Alexander II asked

Louis Roederer to reserve the best cuvée for him, and him alone, every year. And thus Cristal was born.

The special lead crystal bottle? The story goes, that Alexander II was so paranoid about being assassinated he wanted to make sure no one had planted anything in his champagne bottles, which are historically dark, green glass. He wanted a clear glass to be able to check that nothing untoward had been slipped inside. The flat-bottomed crystal bottle is now an icon, as is its orange cellophane wrapper designed to stop the harmful UV rays which a normal green glass bottle would stop. Cristal is one of the most age-worthy champagnes there is, keeping for over 20 years and staying fresh, delicious and developing complexity and flavours, if you have the patience to keep it. As Jean-Baptiste says 'Champagne is time in a bottle. And the true luxury of champagne is time.' I agree, but if I had a bottle of Cristal in my cellar, it wouldn't last long before I popped the cork and drank like a Tsar.

Louis Roederer
Brut Premier

Tasting notes: Orange peel, blood orange and golden apple flavours do the no-pants dance with cream, honeycomb and lemon tarts. Polished, soft and totally delicious. My favourite NV from a major house.

Mixture of steel and oak tanks in the winery mean that Chef du Cave Jean-Baptiste has so many creative options when combining and blending this exceptional champagne, which unlike many NVs will express different qualities each year depending on the vintage. Crafted from 40% Chardonnay, 40% Pinot Noir and 20% Pinot Meunier, blended from six different vintages, with 5% matured in oak, giving this wine richness on the palate. It is of a style which should please all wine and champagne drinkers alike as a true celebration of what a multi-vintage (also known as non-vintage) champagne should taste like. This is the benchmark.

TYPE Multi-Vintage Brut

STYLE Style, joy, seamlessness

PRICE 🍾🍾🍾

STOCKISTS Specialist, high street

TOAST 🍞🍞🍞

FOOD On its own, or with anything

OCCASION All day, everyday

Louis Roederer
Vintage 2009

Tasting notes: Baked plums, Christmas cake spices mingled with crunchy red fruits, fresh raspberries and orange zest. Rich, toasty and round, this champagne combines all the wonderful red apple flavours of Pinot Noir with the zippy, chalky freshness of Chardonnay for a precise and glorious example of what a vintage champagne can be.

This wine is a celebration of Pinot Noir, as Jean-Baptiste makes this wine as Blanc de Noirs (100% Pinot Noir) and then blends in 25% top Chardonnay for salinity and freshness. The Pinot is sourced from Grand Cru vineyards of Verzenay and the Chardonnay from the Côte des Blancs, all sites are top of the pops. The result is a champagne with amazing flavour, and bags of red apple and red berry fruit coming through from the higher Pinot content, paired with the best of Chardonnay of the region. The use of oak, almost 40% of the blend, paired with four years' careful cellaring, means you get extra creamy richness across the palate. The 2009 was a vintage of two halves, a very cold winter followed by a heat wave in summer which results in a stunning year for champagne – and won't be around for ever, stock up when you can.

TYPE Vintage Brut

STYLE Rich, toasted and long

PRICE 🌑🌑🌑🌑

STOCKISTS Specialist, high street

TOAST 🍞🍞🍞

FOOD Roast chicken with all the trimmings

OCCASION Running a sub four hour marathon

Louis Roederer
Cristal 2009

Tasting notes: It doesn't get better than this, an expression of the best vineyards in all of champagne. Precious, harmonious and fresh it ripples and tantalizes with flavours of lemon meringue, chalky salinity, candied fruits, honeycomb and green apples caked in toffee.

Only from the best, chalkiest vineyards of Louis Roederer's 235 hectares, Cristal is a pure expression of the best sites in Champagne. This Pinot dominant champagne is an icon for a reason; it is one of the best wines in the world. It is like drinking silk, soft, flavourful and enduring. It is one of those rare champagnes that when you taste it, you have to stop everything you are doing because you are enveloped in the flavour and pleasure. There is a lot of hype on this wine, believe it! It's in the top three champagnes for me. After six years' careful cellaring the 2009 offers amazing generosity now, unlike some recent other Cristal vintages which means it is drinking beautifully now! But, if you can wait, this wine will cellar incredibly well and show a different expression in 10, 20 years' time: if you are patient you will be rewarded!

TYPE Prestige Cuvée, Vintage Brut

STYLE Top of the Pops

PRICE 🍷🍷🍷🍷🍷

STOCKISTS Specialist

TOAST 🥂🥂🥂

FOOD Something fabulous

OCCASION Lifetime achievement

Moët & Chandon showroom at their HQ, Épernay

Moët & Chandon

moet.com

First off: You pronounce the 'T' in Mo-Ett – it is originally a Dutch name.

You can't talk about the history of champagne without talking about Moët & Chandon. The House is integral to the development and success of champagne and region. Wine and company have grown up and developed together since then Claude Moët established Maison Moët et Cie in 1743 in Épernay, where the company is still based today in an enormous regal palace on Avenue de Champagne.

First off: You pronounce the 'T' in Mo-Ett – it is originally a Dutch name.

Claude was already a man of power and wealth and had huge influence establishing champagne as the drink of choice for nobility and Royalty through his connections in the Royal Courts of Versailles. The French Courts were the epitome of style, culture and sophistication and were the trendsetters of the modern world. This is an important reason why champagne became so desirable, it was the seed of aspiration. When the masses knew their royal family was enjoying Vin Mousseux from Champagne, everyone wanted a taste of the high life.

It was Claude's grandson Jean-Rémy who took the company to the lofty, fizzing heights of success. A noble figure and Mayor of Épernay, Jean Remy had status and gravity when he toured the world selling champagne; the drink of the French Royal Courts and haute culture. He brushed and rubbed lots of shoulders with influential leaders and businessmen across Europe and Russia which opened up new markets and sales channels.

An important factor in securing domestic reputation was the Moët family purchase of the iconic Abbey and vineyards of Hautvillers, the resting place of legendary Dom Perignon. Latterly the Moët family home it was also a status symbol, and the throne of champagne itself. But it wasn't just the Royal courts, his political connections or the Abbey which set Jean-Rémy on the incredible trajectory of success, but his friendship to Napoleon Bonaparte.

The two men met earlier in their careers and became lifelong friends and associates. During any military campaigns Napoleon would always make time to stay in Épernay at the enormous palatial guest house, to be wined and dined on the Avenue de Champagne where the head offices of Moët & Chandon are.

This close relationship made a lot of noise at the time as Napoleon was one of the most famous and influential men in the world, let alone France. Jean-Rémy maximized this celebrity endorsement as powerful marketing leverage. This is when the orders for his champagnes began pouring in so fast he could barely keep up with demand, and the spring board of success the company still enjoys today. For Jean-Rémy's service to France as an International ambassador, representing France while selling champagne and increasing worldwide reputation for French wine Napoleon rewarded his friend with the highest of military awards, the cross of Légion d'Honneur. In response, Moët latterly dedicated their bestselling champagne in Napoleon's

When the masses knew their royal family was enjoying Vin Mousseux from Champagne, everyone wanted a taste of the high life.

honour in 1869, 100 years after his birth. This dedication can still be seen today on every bottle of Brut Imperial.

In 1832, Jean-Rémy handed over the baton to his son Victor and son-in-law, Pierre-Gabriel Chandon de Briailles, and so Moët & Chandon was born.

The legendary Moët & Chandon is celebrating 275 years as the world's most drunk champagne, producing a whopping 30 million bottles a year, almost 10% of the total region's production. People love to hate the biggest kids in the playground, but the quality of wines Moët & Chandon produce is remarkable considering the enormity of the operation under owners LVMH the largest luxury goods firm in the world. Credit is due to Moët & Chandon for their huge marketing budgets however ridiculous! As this constant above-the-line advertising keeps the brand and wines current and has a positive halo effect for all champagne. Although many champagne enthusiasts stay clear of drinking Brut Imperial, the quality and price offers good value and a celebrated name. Merci Moët.

Moët & Chandon
Brut Imperial

Tasting notes: Tastes a lot like champagne, slightly sweet, fruity, very fizzy and refreshing.

A blend of over 100 different wines and components from LVMH's massive vineyard holdings making up almost 6,000 hectares in total. The blend is straight down the middle, 40% Pinot Noir, 40% Pinot Meunier and 20% Chardonnay with up to 30% of reserve wines for depth and consistency. This is often peoples' first taste of champagne, and it is the quality benchmark of the entire region.

TYPE Multi-Vintage Brut

STYLE Starry-eyed people pleaser

PRICE 🍷🍷

STOCKISTS Everywhere

TOAST 🍞

FOOD Late night Chicken Shawarma

OCCASION When bubbles are the only option

G.H. Mumm

mumm.com

❧

Many people's first thought of champagne is the image of Formula 1 racers showering each other and the crowd with bubbles of victory with G.H. Mumm Cordon Rouge on the podium.

The Champagne and racing connection dates back to the 1950s when the first French Grand Prix was held in Reims, and naturally the winner was presented with a bottle of the good stuff. But this dramatic waste of champagne began, like a lot of the best traditions totally by accident! At infamous 24 hour race, Le Mans in 1966 Swiss racer Jo 'Seppi' Siffert accidentally showered the crowd as a bottle of Moët & Chandon burst open spontaneously after it was left out in the sun. The following year American racer Dan Gurney deliberately copied Seppi's action from the year before and so the tradition was born.

This partnership between Mumm and the Grand Prix started in 2000, but came to an end in 2016 when the Mumm's €5 million advertising deal was deemed insufficient. From now on it will be back to the original crowd shower of Moët & Chandon.

Mumm's champagne story starts in Germany in the 1700s, when Peter Arnold Mumm set up a wine merchant in his home town of Cologne. The House we know today was set up by his descendants, three winemaking brothers who took a keen interest in the wines of champagne. So much so, that in 1827 the family set up their own champagne house in Reims.

The emblematic Red Ribbon or 'Cordon Rouge' is in homage to the House's most prestigious clients from the Legion of Honour the highest military order in France, established by Napoleon Bonaparte. The House is now owned by Pernod Ricard, one of the largest drink companies in the world who have big plans for expansion, so expect to see Mumm champagnes more and more on the supermarket shelves.

G.H. Mumm
Cordon Rouge Brut

Tasting notes: Bags of fruit, red apple, and peaches. Sweet fruit profile like a juicy red Macintosh apple, very accessible and lots of spice with touches of cinnamon and nutmeg character. There is a lick of toast, with some cream patisserie flavours, finishing with apricot cream.

A multi-vintage blend of 77 different crus sourced from all over Champagne, this Cordon Rouge is a blend of the three principle champagne grapes; Pinot Noir 45%, Chardonnay 30% and Pinot Meunier 25% with up to 30% reserve wines blended back into for richness and complexity. This Pinot-dominant style gives extra red fruit character and volume across the palate for a really appealing style which all wine lovers, champagne lovers, and podium finishers will enjoy.

TYPE Multi-Vintage Brut

STYLE Apple & peach crumble

PRICE 💷💷

STOCKISTS Supermarkets

TOAST 🍞🍞

FOOD Filo fish parcels with Moroccan spices

OCCASION Mother's Day, obviously

The cellars of G.H. Mumm, Reims

Headquarters of Perrier-Jouët, Avenue de Champagne, Épernay

Perrier-Jouët

perrier-jouet.com

Not many champagne houses are so entwined with haute culture as Perrier-Jouët. Founded in 1811 when Pierre-Nicholas Perrier married 19-year-old beauty Adèle Jouët, they set up shop on the Avenue de Champagne. The House has always been an icon of style, even now under the ownership of drinks conglomerate Pernod Ricard. The wines they produce are accessible and enjoyable, and you don't need to break the bank for their top cuvée expression, the celebrated Belle Epoque.

Belle Epoque, or Beautiful Era was a golden time in French and European history, between the end of the Franco-Prussian War in 1871 and the outbreak of the First World War in 1914. It was a time of peace, economic prosperity, and cultural, artistic and technological revolution. Paris became THE place to be, and many of the iconic pieces of art, music and theatre were created during this period in this epicentre of culture. Post-impressionists like Picasso, Matisse, Gauguin were painting, boozing,

schmoozing and getting creative. Moulin Rouge was in full swing, and the bars of Paris were flowing and swaying with Absinthe and champagne. Art Nouveau was born during this golden age, still celebrated today in the Paris Metro station signs.

It was for this watershed period in culture and creativity that the top cuvée from PJ is named. The House acted as patron to the movement, giving a platform to Émile Gallé, a prominent artist of the time to design a special batch of bottles.

The Japanese anemones engraved into every bottle of Belle Epoque is testament to the Modernist movement celebrating the dawn of the 20th century. This was an important time in France and European history as the emerging middle classes had more money to spend on luxury goods and fine foods, with one increasingly popular drink which encapsulated the current time of prosperity: champagne.

Perrier-Jouët
Belle Epoque 2007

Tasting notes: Tinned peaches, cream and honeysuckle jump from the glass. Nice evolved shortbread character with a mouth full of fruit and berry, zappy freshness and clean length.

Chef du Cave Hervé Deschamps has combined 50% Chardonnay from Grand Cru Cramant and Avize and blended in 45% Pinot Noir from Montagne de Reims with a cheeky splash of Pinot Meunier's 5% from Dizy to round off the blend. Six years' ageing deep in the PJ cellars, means this bottle is bang delicious now, or can be cellared for another ten years.

TYPE Prestige Cuvée, Vintage Brut

STYLE Golden peaches & cream

PRICE 🍷🍷🍷

STOCKISTS High street, specialist

TOAST 🍞🍞🍞

FOOD Cheesy straws, or smoked salmon with cream cheese

OCCASION Family get-together

Pol Roger

polroger.co.uk

Established in 1849, now in the 5th generation of family ownership. Pol keeps true to its principles of unfaltering quality and integrity of style.

Few champagnes are as British as Pol Roger, you will notice the British coat of arms on each bottle. This Royal Warrant means Pol Roger are the purveyors of champagne to the Queen and British Royal Family since 1877. Pol is the Queen's favourite champagne, and the iconic White Foil Brut Réserve was the fizz poured at Kate and Will's wedding. Over the years Pol has carved a reputation as one of the leading, most respected of all Champagne's houses.

Few champagnes are as British as Pol Roger

The Avenue du Champagne in Épernay is Champagne's equivalent to Las Vegas. Travelling down this street is like walking down Champagne's Hall of Fame each house more famous than the last. But the home of Pol Roger is up a little side street tucked away from the immediate hustle and bustle, the address; 1 Rue Winston Churchill.

As for many of the prestige houses, the last 160 years have not been plain

sailing. During the Second World War, the production and buying of champagne was controlled by the Wehrmacht. During the German occupation, certain houses were ordered to give vast quantities of champagne to the Führer, without fail, demanding up to 400,000 bottles of champagne every week. This provided the Resistance with important military intelligence when they started to track the champagne shipments: through the vast orders they could pre-empt where the Germans were preparing to attack next.

Due to these demands of the thirsty Nazis, a number of the champagne houses revolted and sent fake, or shoddy product in place of their usual quality. Some got away with this, but those who were caught were imprisoned or worse. Many champagne houses were threatened with being drunk dry and forced to close. Pol Roger ran this real risk. In 1941, the Comité Interprofessionnel du Vin de Champagne was established to represent the Champenois and protect them as a united front. The CIVC had a collective voice, and helped push back on the unrealistic demands of the Germans from the different champagne cellars. When Pol Roger needed 'urgent repairs' to their winery to meet the German needs, they were supplied with materials and used the cement to wall up and hide their top champagnes!

> 'a single glass of champagne impacts a feeling of exhilaration. The nerves are braced, the imagination is agreeably stirred, the wits become more nimble. A bottle produces the opposite effect'

Pol Roger is a work of love and craftsmanship, and is a fantastic place to visit. The grand House of Pol Roger, which until recently was the family home, sits on top of the polished and clinical winery below. Open the door in the back of the fermentation hall and you are led down to dark and humid chalk cellars, the deepest in Épernay, reaching 33 metres underground in a network of caves and tunnels where eight million bottles of Pol rest quietly before release. What I'd do to get locked in down there...

Churchill was a famous booze hound, and a huge champagne fan. It is said that he even preferred to have his own bottle beside him on the dinner table 'to be independent of the vagaries of butlers'! He famously said 'a single glass of champagne impacts a feeling of exhilaration. The nerves are braced, the imagination is agreeably stirred, the wits become more nimble. A bottle produces the opposite effect'. Well put, Winston. Funny to think that maybe many of the most important decisions in the 20th century were lubricated by a glass of Pol. When Winston met Scottish-born Odette Pol Roger at a Gala lunch after the Paris liberation in 1945, it was the start of a long and fizzy relationship between her, him and her wines. Pol Roger named their top cuvée after their most emphatic customer, and in 1975 Cuvée Winston Churchill was launched. The wines of Pol Roger are, like Churchill himself, independent, definitive and powerful and are some of my favourite champagnes out there. I reckon that if they are good enough for the Queen, they are good enough for the rest of us!

Pol Roger
Brut Réserve 'White Foil'

Tasting notes: Golden straw in colour, the bubbles are fine and attractive. Flavours of pear, mango and white flowers fill the aromas and the palate is bursting with notes of golden apples, honey, vanilla, brioche, quince and zesty tangerine. Long-lasting and layered in flavour.

Pol Roger's flagship is a blend of equal parts of Chardonnay, Pinot Noir and Pinot Meunier sourced from 30 different vineyards all over Champagne, including Grand Cru sites in the Côte des Blancs. It is aged for four years in Pol's 33-metre deep-cellars, adding richness and complexity before release.

TYPE Multi-Vintage Brut

STYLE Strong, silky superiority

PRICE £ £

STOCKISTS High street

TOAST 🍞🍞

FOOD Fish and chips

OCCASION New job, or promotion, or successfully building something from Ikea

Pol Roger
Brut Rosé 2008

Tasting notes: Fresh and intense, red fruits and perfume with wild strawberries and patisserie on the nose. The soft and foaming style of Pol is backed up with grapefruit freshness, married with vanilla, cream and bags of red fruit and Pinot character, almost Burgundian in style. This rosé is ripe, bright and savoury with deep fruit flavour, perfumed and rich and toasted nuts and Mirabelle plum notes. Delicious!

Pol does not make a multi-vintage rosé, so it only made it the best years; 2008 was a wonder harvest in Champagne which meant the Pinot Noir was especially juicy. The blend for Pol rosé is 50% Pinot Noir, 35% Chardonnay with 15% of Pinot Noir vinified red from the famous town of Bouzy, meaning this wine combines the hallmark Pol Roger style, and the true vinous character of great Pinot Noir. Made in limited quantities, and aged in the deep cellars for six-and-a-half years before release.

TYPE Vintage Brut, Rosé

STYLE Seriously pink

PRICE 🍷🍷🍷🍷

STOCKISTS Specialist

TOAST 🍞🍞

FOOD Grilled salmon or a selection of sushi. This rosé would also be wonderful with rhubarb crumble

OCCASION Your anniversary

Pol Roger
Cuvée Sir Winston Churchill 2004

Tasting notes: Intense and complex, this is an incredible champagne of seriousness and total drinkability. Dried fruits, toasted almonds and honey fill your glass. This wine is full-bodied, powerfully flavoured with burnt butter, ripe pear and tart tartan flavours framed by remarkable freshness and citrus edge.

Made only in the best years from a dual blend of Pinot Noir and Chardonnay, sourced from only Grand Cru vineyards which were already producing grapes in Churchill's lifetime. These older vines give rich and complex wines. Careful, slow and extended cellaring mean this wine shows characters which Sir Winston looked for in his wines: full-bodied and relative maturity. As the great man said, *'My tastes are simple. I am easily satisfied with the best.'* With the Cuvée Winston, this is exactly what you're getting.

TYPE Prestige Cuvée, Vintage Brut

STYLE Top of the Pops

PRICE 🍷🍷🍷🍷🍷

STOCKISTS Specialist

TOAST 🍞🍞🍞

FOOD This champagne deserves something special: Pot roast pheasant or cheese fondue

OCCASION Winning at life

Pol Roger showroom, Épernay

Dusty bottles at Charles Heidsieck

Château de Boursault built by the 'Grande Dame of champagne', Madame Clicquot Ponsardin

Pommery

❦

Louise Pommery was another influential woman in Champagne like the infamous Lilly Bollinger or Barbe-Nicole Clicquot, she definitely made her mark. Widowed in 1860 she took her husband's wool and champagne business in the heartland of Reims and, in a relatively short time, spun it into one of the biggest brands of champagne in the world.

Madame Pommery was the first to bring the style we now know as Champagne Brut to the market. Up until the early 1900s champagne was sickly sweet, often containing 200-300 grams of sugar per litre, sweeter than many dessert wines we know today. It was the UK market which prompted this dramatic stylistic change, drier styles were available up until now, but it was Louise who in 1874, after listening to the British customers, launched the first Brut Champagne. The British consumers preferred a lighter, drier style of drink compared to customers in America or Russia, who were also important export markets for champagne at the time. This still holds true today; I notice how sweet the food and drink is when I visit the US, and their wine style preference is no different, they love sugar! We are a little more restrained in the UK, but only just.

The whirlwind success of the Pommery Brut changed champagne forever. Brut Champagne now makes up to 80% of all champagne exports.

The success of this new style meant the Champenois had to get smarter, and change their winemaking to accommodate. Sugar masks faults and off flavours, which means you can get away with sub-standard quality in your wine (or Chinese take-out!) as it hides flavour and our brains are wired to enjoy sweetness.

Madame Pommery was the first to bring the style we now know as Champagne Brut to the market

You will find most of the cheapest wines available in the UK market to contain at least five grams of sugar, as it hides any undesirable characters. Champagne has high acidity, and the historical high sugar content helped balance this aggressive freshness. Without the sweet mask of sugar, champagne became even more technical to make, as the houses had to find other ways to balance the acidity. Grape harvests had to be pushed until later to maximize ripeness and flavour of the grapes, fermentations had to be adapted to soften acidity and ageing had to be done for longer to gain give and richness to the finished wine. All these factors and more have been honed and developed for our drinking enjoyment today.

Nowadays Pommery is part of a large champagne empire, after being sold by LVMH in the 1990s, it is still the seventh largest champagne producer and part of the Vraken-Pommery group. Under Vraken-Pommery they have lost some of their original charm. However, they make some of the best value champagne in the market and are a good option when you're not feeling plush or have a lot of thirsty drinkers coming round.

Madame Pommery commissioned sculptor Gustave Navlet
to carve spectacular bas-reliefs in the cellars' chalk walls

Pommery
Brut Royal

Tasting notes: White cherry, apples and pears dominate the fresh and foaming style. Light and very fizzy, what this champagne lacks in complexity is made up by a red apple sweetness and drinkability which drinkers can too easily fall for.

Blend of the three classic champagne grapes, aged for three years in the dark 18 km worth of cellars under the City of Reims. This is a people-pleasing style and great bang for buck.

TYPE Multi-Vintage Brut

STYLE Fizzy party juice

PRICE 🄯🄯

STOCKISTS Supermarkets

TOAST 🍞🍞

FOOD Simple nibbles and finger food

OCCASION Staff party, please don't cause a scene

Ruinart

ruinart.com

Ruinart is the world's oldest champagne house, founded by Dom Ruinart's nephew Nicolas in 1729. This was one year after Louis XV allowed champagne houses to sell their wine in bottles from 1728, opening up export trade and changing champagne forever.

There was a common denominator for the young and entrepreneurial Champenois, who were some of the original travelling salesmen – charisma. Young Nicolas was an ambitious and talented man, full of beans, charm and flair. Sparkling wine was a brand new product at the time young Nicolas was trying to flog it around Europe, Russia and latterly the USA. Champagne houses have some of the strongest brand equity for any winery or product on the planet, and you need great communication skills and a strong story to persuade customers to spend £30+ on a bottle. Champagne's branding and marketing nowadays, although sometimes over the top, is the legacy of these few intrepid salesmen who first started to market their wines directly to consumers.

There are two famous Doms in Champagne. The underdog is Dom Thierry Ruinart. Legend has it that the two monks were good pals up in the spiritual home of champagne, the Abbey of Hautvillers, and

Pierre told Thierry all his juicy secrets. If Dom Perignon was the first man to understand the pressing and blending of champagne, it was Dom Ruinart who began to age champagne properly. He did this for this first time in the Roman chalk mines in the local capital of Reims. These 'crayères' are the perfect place for storing and maturing champagne.

The champagne rests and develops underground with no natural light, no vibrations and a yearly constant temperature of around 10C. Ruinart's chalk cellars are the deepest and most spectacular in the whole of champagne, tunnelling 38 meters below the streets of Reims, and are the only cellars in the whole world to have UNESCO World Heritage status.

Champagne's branding and marketing nowadays, although sometimes over the top, is the legacy of these few intrepid salesmen

Ruinart is now part of the luxury goods conglomerate LVMH, the humble one on the team sheet behind Moët, Veuve and Krug – but by no means is it lesser.

The man at the helm is now smooth talking Frédéric Panaiotis, a self-acclaimed fiend for Chardonnay. Ruinart is all about Chardonnay, which is the golden thread which links the Ruinart taste across their wines, their Blanc de Blancs is the benchmark of champagne, portrayed in their iconic 18th century bell-shaped bottle, a nod to their long history. Their top splash, the Prestige Cuvée Dom Ruinart is one of the best Blanc de Blancs there is.

What I also like about Ruinart is that they are one of the few major champagne houses that is drunk more in France than exported

What I also like about Ruinart is that they are one of the few major champagne houses that is drunk more in France than exported, a good gauge in quality, as the French have been drinking it for almost 300 years.

Ruinart
Dom Ruinart 2004

Tasting notes: Pure expression of champagne's top Chardonnay, this exquisite Blanc des Blancs sings with candied citrus fruit, gun powder and glorious, toasted expression. Oatcakes, butterscotch, marmalade and buttered, toasted brioche combine with riveting chalky freshness.

100% Grand Cru Chardonnay, this is one of the most famous expressions of pure Chardonnay in Champagne and the House's flagship wine. A mixture of Côte des Blancs for purity, freshness and longevity and blended with fruit from Montagne de Reims which gives it a more unctuous and riper style of Blanc de Blancs. Aged peacefully in the UNESCO cellars for ten years before release. This champagne is worth robbing a bank for!

"Chardonnay is both the golden thread of Ruinart and also the soul of the House"

— *Frédéric Panaiotis, Cellar Master*

TYPE Prestige Cuvée, Vintage Brut, Blanc de Blancs

STYLE Golden, fruity and rich

PRICE 🆒🆒🆒🆒🆒

STOCKISTS Specialist

TOAST 🍞🍞🍞🍞

FOOD Pan roasted John Dory

OCCASION Life's big milestones

Ruinart
Blanc de Blancs

Tasting notes: Light and fruity with bags of apple, ripe pear and Starburst lemon and lime. Subtle spices like cayenne and white pepper flirt on the palate with floral honeysuckle and flashes of grapefruit. Super fresh, super clean, super delicious.

Blend of many different Chardonnay components from Montagne de Reims and Côte des Blancs this is one of the benchmark styles of Blanc de Blancs. A blend of three different vintages, and 25% reserve wines. This champagne will develop round and nutty flavours if you are patient enough to age it. If you do, keep it out of direct sunlight as the clear bottle looks stylish, but doesn't offer any UV protection and it would be a shame to waste it!

TYPE Multi-Vintage Brut, Blanc de Blancs

STYLE Apple, pears and flair

PRICE 🄫🄫

STOCKISTS High street

TOAST 🍞🍞

FOOD Eggs Benedict

OCCASION Breakfast of champions

Salon

salondelamotte.com

You could easily walk right past it, tucked up on a top street of the village, directly backing on to the slope of the Côte des Blancs is a greasy brass plaque on the gabled gate reading Champagne A. Salon & Cie, Le Mesnil.

This picturesque wee town is a destination in every champagne lover's map, built on a bedrock of pure chalk which rises to the surface on the slope behind Mesnil's winding streets towards the top of the Côte des Blancs behind. The vineyards of this town are widely recognized as being some of the finest Chardonnay vineyards in the world, for the vines' rampant love affair with chalk.

For champagne producers it's a postcode you want on your address as the quality of the wines here is outstanding, and carry a certain cachet. Many of the top, most expensive champagnes in the region will be made from a proportion from this area, you can taste it in the wines. Every winemaker from the region wants wines from here to blend into their own as it produces wines with more salinity and longevity than anywhere else.

Champagne growers can charge an extra premium for the wine here, not only because of the quality of the wines, but also due to the reputation of one estate whose champagnes are some of the most

sought after and expensive in the world. This is Champagne Salon.

Salon has had more to do with putting the Mesnil-sur-Oger on the winemaking map than any other producer in the town due to its exceptional expression of single vineyard Chardonnay. You might wonder what all the fuss is about when you walk up the leg-aching hill past Salon and peer across the single plot of vines or Jardin de Salon directly behind the house. Both building and vineyard appear very modest – a far cry from the tourist-friendly big houses, but there be magic in those vines.

A short distance from le Jardin is a tree-lined grotto where people have taken pilgrimages for centuries in search of miracles. Carved into stone in the grotto overlooking Salon and adjacent vineyards, names, dates and descriptions of performed miracles stare back at you, many from the war which was fought in the very vineyards of champagne. Whether you are a pilgrim, wine lover or teetotaler you can really feel that this particular part of the world is special.

Founder Eugene-Aimé Salon pioneered Champagne's first ever Blanc de Blancs in the early 1900s. The famous branded 'S' on Salon bottles represents a single wine, a single grape, a single vineyard, a single time and one man's singular vision. He was a driven man with one mission; in search of the holy coupe! He searched and searched but couldn't find a champagne with the class, power or grace he was looking for, so he created it himself.

The vineyards of this town are widely recognized as being some of the finest Chardonnay vineyards in the world, for the vines' rampant love affair with chalk.

Originally only destined for personal consumption, the first commercial vintage was in 1921. Since then many producers have followed suit but few rarely reach the pinnacle of the style as Salon. Nowadays the mystique is slightly diluted, but by no means less special, as Laurent Perrier own and produce both Salon and Delamotte.

For champagne connoisseurs Salon is the world's most sought after champagne, it is the quintessential Blanc de Blancs and an icon of this style. This legendary champagne House only produces one champagne, and only ever one. Unlike many of the Prestige Cuvées you find in high end nightclubs around the world,

you wouldn't dare see anyone pour Salon anywhere except into an appropriate champagne glass. For all champagne drinkers and gastronomes, Salon needs to be tasted at some point in your life.

They age the wines for at least ten years before releasing their Vintage – only made in the finest years, an average three per decade. Everything in the production is for the long game, keeping the style of Salon separate from the earlier drinking style of brother-maison Delamotte across the road. If you do find a bottle, which is difficult and expensive, put it away for another few years, and when you get round to opening it, pray it isn't corked!

Côte des Blancs vineyards

Salon
Le Mesnil Grand Cru 2002

Tasting notes: The aromas are lifted and layered with white flowers, ginger, honeysuckle and toasted hazelnuts. The palate is a tightrope walk of chalk, backed by orange and candied citrus, freshly buttered croissants and sea spray salinity, sensual chaos. Over the years this champagne will transform into a spectacle celebration of Chardonnay, gaining richness in texture and weight, showcasing one of the greatest vineyards on the planet, and the longevity and quality of wines which hail from it.

2002 was an epic vintage in Champagne. All the wines you see from '02 have power, chew and richness whilst keeping great freshness. The Salon 2002 is in a fetal stage right now: it has tension and concentration on the palate which will help it age to 2060 and beyond. These wines are not forthcoming in their youth, they need time to open, develop and evolve. The Maison suggests a drinking age of 20-30 years.

TYPE Prestige Cuvée, Vintage Brut, Blanc de Blancs

STYLE If you wait, you shall be rewarded

PRICE 🍷🍷🍷🍷🍷

STOCKISTS Very specialist

TOAST 🍞🍞

FOOD Your desert island dish

OCCASION Your 100th birthday

Jacques Selosse

selosse-lesavises.com

❧❧

Pioneers are few and far between in Champagne today, but Anselme Selosse is definitely one of them. After taking over the family firm from his dad in the 80s, his eccentric out-of-the-box approach has turned many heads, many in favour and some in disagreement.

But a producer with his own vision is a breath of fresh air in an industry dominated by uniform styles, big brands and marketing budgets. Even if people don't like this approach and funky wine style, nobody could disagree with the personality of the champagnes.

The demand for his tiny annual productions of terroir-driven styles means prices are sky-rocketing as these wines are the crème de la crème for collectors, avid enthusiasts and top-end restaurants. But when you manage to track down and pop open a bottle, you will understand why you just broke your piggybank.

His philosophy to making wine is more akin to the most expensive Burgundian wine, a couple of hundred miles south of Champagne. His visionary approach to the land he farms, lowering the yields of grapes produced to get the best concentration and expression per vine, and his biodynamic farming principles mean his champagnes are some of the most expressive and flavoursome in

all of the region. For some traditional champagne drinkers, his wines carry some funky flavours as he walks a tightrope of style versus oxidation. I love wines which polarize, and I'm firmly on the favourable side of the fence.

If you are looking for a unique and exciting bottle of champagne, you can't beat the wines of Selosse.

Vineyard expression is everything to Selosse, the entirety of what he does is to express the land and anything which might interfere with the natural balance of the ecosystem is severely avoided.

Although Selosse wouldn't be pigeon-holed as biodynamic, many of the principles he follows are within the realms. Biodynamic viticulture stems from its suggestions of Rudolf Steiner, who spearheaded the movement in the 1920s. The principles of biodynamics seem totally crazy for most, but many of the best wines in the world are produced following these methods, including much of Louis Roederer Champagne, Domaine Zind-Humbrecht in Alsace, Domaine Romanée-Conti in Burgundy and Château Pontet-Canet in Bordeaux.

The principles of biodynamics are based on the cosmic and lunar rhythms of the universe and balance of the farm's ecosystem. This sounds like total gobbledygook at first, but it involves many ancient practical farming practices including planting and farming in time with lunar cycles, encouraging natural vigour in the vineyards and avoiding any unnatural or harmful agricultural sprays or pesticides. Opposed to treating vines when needed, biodynamic practices encourage farmers to manage their farm as its own ecosystem, encouraging roots to grow deeper, and wildlife, plants and vines to be healthier.

Biodynamic wine is organic wine on natural steroids, on a slightly hippy level. Many biodynamic wines are funky, oxidized and weird-tasting – this isn't because of the quality of the fruit, but often the minimalist or dinosaur wine making methods used.

The principles of biodynamics are based on the cosmic and lunar rhythms of the universe

Natural and biodynamic wines are not an excuse for faulty, lazy or poor winemaking which can be the case and is a brush with which biodynamic wines are often painted – this is not the case for Selosse. His controversial wines have kick-started a huge movement in the whole of champagne to respect and express the terroir, and have empowered the voice of the individual grower rather than just the Grande Marques and bottlers.

This farming practice manifests itself with intensity, minerality and flavour of the finished wine. These practices don't stop in the vineyards; the attention and principles of nurturing quality are taken through vinification and winemaking. Selosse is one of the most respected men in Champagne today, and many of the Chefs du Cave I've met have mentioned him as an example of a man who knows no compromise in the quest of quality and expression, and he isn't bothered about chucking out the rule book to do so. If you are looking for a unique and exciting bottle of champagne, you can't beat the wines of Selosse.

his champagnes are some of the most expressive and flavoursome in all of the region

His approach to winemaking is just as unique as his farming, using oak barrels to ferment his grapes, impacting flavour and texture in the finished styles, this also opens the wines up to oxygen which has a huge effect on the finished champagne style, and you will notice Selosse's champagne to be a richer, golden hue because of it.

The wines of Selosse are expressive and taste totally unique to the place where they are made. Like all of the greatest wines in the world, the best are never generic. If you are looking to impress, collect a champagne for investment or just buy a very special bottle; you have just found your new favourite producer.

Vineyards in Marne, Champagne

Jacques Selosse
VO. Grand Cru Blanc de Blancs

Tasting notes: Massively intense, candied fruit, Bakewell tarts, sweet, waxy and floral, smoky and exuberant which follows through to aromas of toasted nuts, vanilla and orange blossom, oxidative and rich. The palate is gleaming and fleshy, with a mouth filling viscosity, soft foam and intense freshness. Mineral, exotic and dangerously moreish. Mega!

The Version Originale is a multi-vintage blend, based on three separate years; 2009, 2008 and 2007 vintages, from three different sites across the Côte des Blancs; Avize, Oger & Cramant. The base wine was fermented on old oak barrel, impacting flavour and texture to the finished style, this also opens the wines up to oxygen which has a huge effect on flavour and appearance, you will notice Selosse's champagnes are a richer, golden hue because of it. Natural yeast is used for both first and second fermentation, which again adds texture and a savoury character to the wines. And Like Clouet, he uses a solera system for his reserve wines, just like sherry – this again adds complexity to the finished style. Then, aged for up to 42 months in cellar, impacting even more rich character! Whilst retaining the mineral backbone from the exceptional Grand Cru Chardonnay. Very dry, with less than 1 gram of sugar a bottle means you taste every element from the vineyard terroir, his unique winemaking and extended cellaring for a party on your palate.

TYPE Multi-Vintage Extra Brut

STYLE Yellow golden galaxy

PRICE 💷💷💷💷💷

STOCKISTS Specialist

TOAST 🥂🥂🥂🥂

FOOD Bresse Chicken, basted in butter and cep mushrooms

OCCASION Your deathbed

Taittinger

Taittinger.com

Taittinger are one of the oldest and most famous champagne houses, founded in 1734 and are a considerable force as the region's sixth largest producer. For their size and wide distribution the real quality stacks up, and they are reliable and consistent across the board. They make a range of styles, including the new disco-ball looking Nocturne, which is perfect for glitzy nightclubs or a girls' night in. Their flagship Comtes de Champagne Blanc de Blancs is a different story all together, and is a serious step above any other of their range. It is one of the most consistent and desirable of all champagnes, a favourite of mine from my sommelier days.

One of the most consistent and desirable of all champagnes

The emblem used as the Taittinger logo is as ancient as the region of champagne itself, and could be something out of a Dan Brown novel! It was used by the first Count of champagne or 'Comte de Champagne' – Hugh the First, who ruled the region in the 11th century and was a member of the Knights Templar, which was founded in the Champagne region.

The company is now part of a larger commercial enterprise, but still partially owned by the original Taittinger family. Run by President Pierre-Emmanuel Taittinger, son Clovis and daughter Vitalie, who are all involved day to day in the Taittinger empire.

If England needed any more endorsements for its quality wines, it is when the champagne producers are looking over the channel for vineyards! With annual production at 4.5 million bottles in 2016, English wine is anything but novelty; some outstanding wines are being made and the quality is only getting better. Taittinger are the first champagne producer to invest in vines in the South of England, buying a majority share of land in Kent, which goes to show that we may be drinking even more sparkling English wines in the years to come.

Taittinger
Comtes de Champagne 2006

Tasting notes: Floral, honey, elegant fruit of lemons, candy apple, pear prickled with cloves. The toast factor comes through as oat meal and honey which is finished with classic Côte des Blancs Chardonnay character of chalk, sea shells and smoke.

2006 was a hot year which translated into fruit and openness in the champagne style. 100% Chardonnay, only sourced from prime-time vineyards down the Côte des Blancs including Avize and Le Mesnil-sur-Oger, this is a true benchmark of Blanc de Blancs. Aged in the deep chalk cellars in Reims from eight to ten years before release this Chardonnay evolves richness and toasted brioche character which is accentuated by a proportion of the blend which is aged in oak barrel, just like a fine Burgundian Chardonnay. This is drinking like a boss now, but will develop and mature for 10 to 20 years no problem.

TYPE Prestige Cuvée, Vintage Brut, Blanc de Blancs

STYLE Bright, peachy and fresh

PRICE £££££

STOCKISTS High street

TOAST 🍞🍞

FOOD Poached chicken breast, crispy, salted skin and picked mushrooms

OCCASION Graduation dinner

Veuve Clicquot

veuveclicquot.com

We know Dom Perignon and praise him for his influence in creating champagne, but there is one other who we should give special thanks too, not only for developing the champagne-making method, but also revolutionizing how champagne is sold, branded and marketed around the world. This legend is Veuve Clicquot.

Barbe-Nicole Ponsardin was a child of the French Revolution, an unassuming girl from an aristocratic family of wool merchants in Reims. She had been born with bubbles in her blood, as her grandmother was the daughter of Nicolas Ruinart, the nephew of legendary Dom Thierry Ruinart. Nicolas founded the world's first champagne house in 1729. So, you could say that Barbe-Nicole's destiny was to revolutionize the industry which her great grandfather had started in the first place!

As was often the case in those days, she was raised to be a wife and a mother, to be married off into a correct family for economic reasons rather than love. The lucky man was François Clicquot, a man who was already part of a family wine company in Reims. But as fortune would have it, she was left widowed before the age of 30 with a young daughter to care for. In 1806, after the death of her husband, 'Widow' Madame Clicquot renamed her company Veuve Clicquot Ponsardin & Co and against all odds, without training, and with only narrow experience, she took the small family wine firm which she had shared with her late husband, and transformed it into one of the greatest champagne houses in the world. She revolutionized the selling and making of champagne, whilst empowering the women of the modern world to follow her example at a time when women in business were unheard of. Without Veuve Clicquot, champagne wouldn't be what we know it as today.

against all odds, without training, and with only narrow experience, she took the small family wine firm which she had shared with her late husband, and transformed it into one of the greatest champagne houses in the world

The wines that Barbe-Nicole and her husband François first sold were sweet and looked nothing like the champagne we know today: even the best wines in the region at the time were muddy pink and very murky. A perfectionist, she wasn't content with the hue of the champagnes being drunk and knew many of her customers weren't either. So with her cellar master they pioneered two vital champagne making methods: riddling & disgorgement which changed champagne from the murky shades of the time, to the gleaming clear wine we know today. But before Barbe-Nicole had her way, all those yeasty lees stayed in the bottle, giving the wine a cloudy appearance. Disgorgement is the removal of the lees from the champagne, cleaning the appearance of champagne and making room for the sugary dosage, which is what houses add back in to each bottle after the lees and some inevitable spillage have been removed. The dosage will be made of sugar, reserve wines and sometimes brandy, which the London bar owners added to their barrels. This had a profound effect on the finished wine style, and these factors transformed champagne. It hugely improved the overall quality of the wine, it meant that houses had more control of the style, it gave clarity to the wine in the glass and drastically enhanced the final taste. But it wasn't only the riddling and disgorgement which Barbe-Nicole had the foresight of developing, but also rosé.

Not content enough with the transformation of the clarity of the wine, she decided to blend a proportion of the local red wine back into the champagne, to give it colour and wine-like flavours which launched in 1818. It wasn't an overnight success but it was the start of a whole new category.

1811 was a poignant vintage for Veuve Clicquot. At the time of the vintage, the sky was filled by the flight of a star-light comet which many thought of as a good luck charm. Veuve Clicquot did and the quality of the harvest of 1811 in Champagne turned out to be the best champagne anyone had ever tasted.

Up until now, champagnes were sold with trust, as there was little way to differentiate between different champagnes since there were no labels or branding, just blank bottles. With the good fortune from the comet vintage, Madam Clicquot branded each cork with a comet and star. You will find many different champagnes even now use comets and stars in their branding in recognition and respect for Madame Clicquot and the vin de la comète. With her personalized corks, Madame Clicquot had developed the first brand in the whole of champagne, years before her iconic Yellow Label was introduced.

The luck of the comet didn't last long! In 1814 the Russians invaded, capturing her home city of Reims. Madame Clicquot hid her precious Comet Vintage deep in her chalky cellars, being the smart lady she was, and went on the charm offensive and offered the Russians a less good champagne before they broke down her doors. The invasion didn't last long, and once the French army had recaptured Reims, it was France's turn to celebrate. Drinking on horseback and dancing in the streets lopping off the champagne bottle necks with swords while riding through town – sounds like a lot of fun! This tradition of cutting off the necks of champagne bottles is know widely known as sabrage and is still done today, even with an iPhone!

But it was actually the Russians who helped elevate Veuve Clicquot to fame and fortune, as well as genius intuition from Madame Clicquot herself. At the beginning of the 19th century borders between France and Russia were closed and trade had been blocked due to the war. But news of Madame Clicquot's magic sparkling elixir was spread by the Russian soldiers who made it back from France alive. With peace on the horizon, Madame Clicquot chartered a ship across the Baltic Sea which arrived into Russia the day the trade block lifted, no other producer had the insight to do this. This meant that Veuve's champagne was the only champagne available at the very time when Russians were celebrating. Her champagne was lapped up and the 1811 comet vintage which she had hidden from the Russian soldiers in her hometown was now making her rich and famous across Russia and Europe.

By 1830, Madame Clicquot was a household name and her now labelled champagne was now exported with a white label into the UK, Russia, Prussia, Europe and the USA. By the 1860s champagne was big business, and again, it was we Brits who asked for a drier style of champagne. A new cuvée was introduced to cater for our needs, and so the now iconic Yellow label was launched in 1877.

Veuve Clicquot is now the second largest champagne house there is, behind mammoth Moët & Chandon, also owned by LVMH. But considering they produce 18 million bottles a year, the quality is truly exceptional. For an operation of such enormity, the quality of the wines is astonishing. The trademark Yellow Label champagne oozes with richness, character and fullness of fruit in the gushing forward style of the house. But, the real comets of the range are the vintage styles which are named after the great woman of champagne, La Grande Dame, which rival any prestige cuvée in the region.

Veuve Clicquot
Brut Yellow Label

Tasting notes: Golden yellow with white fruits, raisins, vanilla and brioche. Fruity and toasty, with a hint of spice.

The use of large oak vats is an important feature for Veuve, the wine sees one year in wood giving the style of Yellow label roundness and texture in the mouth, opposed to immediate oaky flavours. Blended from around 60 different vineyards, with a dominance of Pinot Noir in the blend. It is then blended with a third of Veuve's special reserve wines, which are Veuve's secret for success and flavour; the age of some of the reserve wines is 30 years old, which adds greater complexity and roundness to the wines in generous Veuve style.

"The Veuve Clicquot style is based on the Pinot Noir, a dominant grape variety in our blends. Yellow Label, our flagship, represents the essence of the Veuve Clicquot style: A vibrant wine with strength, power and structure, balanced by a tremendous complexity, dominated by fruits and brioche flavour."

– Dominique Demarville, Cellar Master

TYPE Multi-Vintage Brut

STYLE Fruity, toasty, tasty

PRICE 🍷🍷🍷

STOCKISTS Everywhere

TOAST 🍞🍞🍞

FOOD Party Bellinis and Parmesan couchettes

OCCASION Trying to forget 2016 happened

Veuve Clicquot
Demi-Sec

Tasting notes: Bags of sweet flavour; yellow melon, candied lemons and frosted flakes. Sweet and ripe across the palate, smooth, fruity and toasted.

This is the original sweet style of champagne, and the original white label from Veuve Clicquot. The sweetness sits at the modest 45g/l, compared to that of 200g or more of the 1900s! Despite the sweetness this carries, it is still a quintessential Veuve style champagne with a dominance of Pinot Noir in the blend, with an increased proportion of Pinot Meunier for extra fruit flavour. With the higher level of sugar, this wine will age very well. The longer you leave it maturing, the more praline, nutty and biscuit notes it will develop.

TYPE Multi-Vintage Demi-Sec (semi sweet)

STYLE Sweet fruit dessert

PRICE 🄲🄲🄲

STOCKISTS Specialist

TOAST 🍞🍞🍞

FOOD Cheese! Fruit-based desserts; macaroons, white chocolate mousse, panna cotta and berry compote, Tarte Tatin or Crêpe Suzette. I'm getting hungry!

OCCASION After dinner treat

Veuve Clicquot
La Grande Dame 2006

Tasting notes: Sparkling gold. Full-bodied, a generous style with bags of flavour.White cherries, red apple compote on shortbread, with a mineral, chalky back palate. Long, persistent finish which just makes you wanna drink more of it!

This is the flagship wine of Veuve Clicquot, made from vineyards which Madame Clicquot would have known herself from eight traditional Grands Crus, arguably some of the best sites in the whole region. I love the Veuve Clicquot wines across the board, but you really do pay for what you get here: the quality is outstanding. Pinot dominant which gives this wine roundness and fruit intensity, while the small amount of Chardonnay, sourced exclusively from the Barbe-Nicole's own vineyard in Oger in the Côte des Blancs, gives freshness, salinity and direction. This is an exceptional champagne, worthy of cellaring. If I had a bottle in my cellar, I wouldn't open it for at least another five years.

TYPE Prestige Cuvée, Vintage Brut

STYLE Classy, fruity, silky

PRICE ●●●●

STOCKISTS Specialist

TOAST 🍞🍞🍞

FOOD Fuller fish dishes; shellfish, monkfish, John Dory. Langoustines with lemongrass

OCCASION Your mum's birthday, go on, treat her!

Virginie T

champagneviriniet.com

Brand new champagne houses are a rarity in such a historic region. So it took some courage for Virginie Taittinger to leave the family firm and strike out on her own to establish Virginie T Champagne in 2007. Based in Sillery, the town where one of the first ever champagnes was produced, this tiny family-run operation is a serious champagne producer and one to watch. Virginie was a model in her youth, and came from a strong stock of Champenois: her mother's family owned champagne Piper-Heidsieck, and her father was Claude Taittinger of champagne Taittinger fame.

So when Virginie had a minor disagreement with her cousin, now owner of Taittinger Champagne and decided to go it alone, she was in a good position to start up afresh. Luckily for us, she was in good favour with her family's best grape growers who followed her to her new house, which explains the generosity and intensity of her styles.

The Grande Cuvée 6 Year also comes in an innovative gift box, which opens up like a flower into a portable ice bucket. Genius! The wine itself is rich and complex, aged in their new cellars for six years until it was bottled in March 2015, and is developing incredible flavour and richness.

This is new school champagne from an up and coming producer. It isn't vintage specific, rather multi-vintage and multi-varietal which really means there are more options for Virginie to create the best wine she can. The Virginie T style is round, rich and smooth combining the best of her Grand Cru contacts and careful ageing. It is a small operation, which means overheads are low and offers great value – a wine of this quality could easily be twice the price if it were produced by a larger name. These smaller houses are really exciting, and I'm looking forward to seeing what Virginie T and the other smaller names are going to launch in the coming years, Champagne is such a historic region and wine so I get very excited when there are new kids on the block.

Virginie T
6 Year Old Grande Cuvée

Tasting notes: Seamless, rich and foaming. Round and fine with intense, ripe and ready fruit style. Some sweet spice thrown into the mixer with cinnamon, tobacco and cocoa. Long and forthcoming, drinking well right now with a spiced, candied pineapple finish.

70% of Pinot Noir, 20% Chardonnay and 10% Pinot Meunier all from Grand and Premier Cru sites across the Champagne region. This Pinot dominant style gives weight and richness, which oozes pleasure when you drink. This is a blend from 2008, an outstanding vintage, blended with 15% of reserve cuvée from the 2007 harvest for complexity and balance.

TYPE Multi-Vintage Brut

STYLE Generous, soft and pretty

PRICE 🌰🌰🌰

STOCKISTS Online

TOAST 🍞🍞🍞

FOOD Scallops with pork fat or crispy udon noodles

OCCASION You've got a bonus and it's party time

Glossary

A

Appellation (AOC) – A defined area of French wine production with its own rules and regulations.

Assemblage – The blending of base wines or Vins Clairs to create champagne.

Autolysis – The technical term for the toasted, biscuit and creamy flavours which develop in champagne after ageing in bottle. This is due to the enzymatic breakdown of yeast cells following the second fermentation. See Toast.

B

Barrique (or Barrels) – Were historically used for transporting or storing wine, but now used for intended maturing or ageing. Fermenting or maturing wine in oak barrels gives rounder texture and flavours of spice, vanilla, wood, coffee and sweet oxidative notes.

Blanc de Blancs – Champagne made from 100% Chardonnay.

Blanc de Noirs – A champagne made from 100% black grapes; usually Pinot Noir or Pinot Meunier or a combination of the two.

Bouquet – Not flowers! The aroma of champagne.

Brut – French term for a dry champagne with a little sweetness. A Brut champagne must have less than nine grams of sugar a bottle and is the most popular style, making up 90% of all champagne production.

Brut Nature – Also called Zero Dosage, Pas Dosage or Ultra Brut! These champagnes have no added sugar, meaning they are bone dry and extra fresh.

C

CIVC (Comité Interprofessionnel du Vin de Champagne) – The Organization which represents, rules and regulates champagne.

Chalk – Chalk is the main soil component which gives champagne its unique quality.

Chardonnay – White grape accounts for 30% of all champagne production.

Clos – Single vineyard.

Cru – Designation of a village where champagne is produced, there are 319 registered villages or (Crus) in Champagne.

Crémant – A French sparkling wine, often made using the same technique and same grapes as champagne production but outside the Champagne region.

Cuvée – Not delimited to any particular style champagne, cuvée is a blend which makes a specific type of champagne. Often used to name a blend, i.e. Bollinger's Special Cuvée.

Cuvée de Prestige – A house's most prestigious and expensive champagne.

Coupe – Breast-shaped wine glass.

Côte des Blancs – Bang tidy area of champagne located south of Épernay. It has some of the finest vineyards in the whole of the region and is famous for the production of Chardonnay due to its high chalk content.

Crayères – Chalk cellars, typically used for ageing and maturing champagne. Some of these incredible cellars were originally built by the Romans and are still in use today.

D

Demi-Sec – Half-sweet style of champagne, containing up to 37.5 grams of sugar per bottle.

Disgorgement – The removal of the lees in the neck of the bottle following the riddling process. This important process in champagne production was developed by Veuve Clicquot.

Dosage – The 'dose' of sugar added to champagne after disgorgement which will affect the final level of sweetness of a champagne.

Doux – Sweet style of champagne, containing more than 37.5 grams of sugar a bottle.

E

Extra Brut – Champagne style containing less than 4.5 grams of sugar per bottle.

Épernay – The Capital of champagne, located directly in the centre of the region is home to some of the most famous houses: Moët & Chandon, Mercier, Pol Roger, Perrier Jouet amongst others. Épernay's Avenue de Champagne is a boulevard of grand proportions, and Champagne's most famous address. It is said to be the most expensive road in the world for the millions and millions of champagne bottles which rest quietly in the cellars below the street.

F

Fermentation – The process of yeast eating sugar, turning into alcohol & carbon dioxide.

Flute – A popular sparkling wine glass which looks pretty but impedes the quality of champagne.

G

Grand Cru – Designates the best class of vineyards in the whole of champagne. Out of 319 listed villages in the region only 17 have this Grand status.

Grande Marque – The largest and most famous champagne houses who have strict quality standards. Out of the 300 champagne houses in the region, only 24 are classified as Grande Marque. Grande Marques will own vineyards, but often buy in grapes from growers each vintage.

Grower Champagne – A champagne grown and bottled by a single estate. Grower champagnes tend to be produced in small quantities and often don't confirm to the traditional styles of a Grande Marque.

H

Hautvillers – The Benedictine Abbey and the spiritual home of champagne, and final resting place of Dom Perignon.

L

Lees – The deposit of dead yeast cells following fermentation. The time a wine is in contact with lees will impact the toasty flavours of the champagne.

M

Malolactic fermentation – A biochemical process which transforms malic acids (green apple) to lactic acids (crème fraîche). There is no right or wrong regarding malo vs. non-malo champagne styles, both will create different styles.

Millésime – A vintage year of champagne, if a vintage is written on the label 100% of the wine must come from that year. Vintage champagnes is not an indication of quality, but champagne houses only produce vintage wines in good years so expect a Millésime champagne to be a high standard. Millésime champagnes benefit from extended ageing, if you can wait. See Vintage.

Minerality – A common wine descriptor which isn't even in the dictionary! It refers to the sapidity and salinity of a wine. In champagne it translates into flavours of chalk, wet stone and the mineral soils where the champagne is grown.

Méthode Champenoise – The correct term for the champagne-making method, also called Traditional Method outside of the Champagne region. It denotes sparkling wine which has had second fermentation in bottle, correct ageing, riddling and disgorgement.

Montagne de Reims – Key sub-zone of champagne, in the hilly district situated between Reims and Épernay. Famous for its chalky soils, it produces some of the best wines in the whole region. The dominant grape variety is Pinot Noir.

Mousse – The fizz of champagne! The mousse is the effervescence of champagne or sparkling wine. The best mousse should have small, foaming and persistent bubbles, exploding with flavour without being aggressively fizzy.

Multi-Vintage – See Non-Vintage.

N

Non-Vintage (NV) – The most common of champagnes. NVs are a blend of multiple years of champagne to maintain a consistent style and quality year after year. I prefer to call them Multi-Vintage champagnes. Most NVs will be released ready to drink, but benefit from a further six months' cellaring, if you have the patience! NV is not an indication of quality, as they can be produced at many different quality levels.

P

Phylloxera – A vine pest, originating in North America which spread itself around the world in the 1800s and destroyed 99% of vineyards across Europe. It arrived in Champagne in the 1890s and devastated the vineyards. There are still some pre-phylloxera vines in Champagne which are extremely rare and make very expensive champagnes.

Pinot Noir – The flagship red grape of champagne, and the most challenging to grow. Pinot Noir also produces some of the best and most prized red wine on the planet, famously in nearby Burgundy. Pinot Noir accounts for over 38% of all Champagne vines.

Pinot Meunier – Often thought of as the lesser of the champagnes' grapes, which shouldn't be the case. It is Champagne's second most planted red grape, accounting for 32% of all vineyard area and gives yellow plum and fruity flavours to champagne.

Punt – The indentation on the bottom of a wine bottle and not an indication of quality!

Press – The apparatus to press the grapes to release the juice from the fruit.

Premier Cru – This is the second best quality class of all villages in the region. 42 out of the 319 have Premier Cru status.

Reims – The heart of the Champagne region, and the official capital of the Champagne-Ardenne region. Home to many of the most famous champagne producers including Veuve, Charles Heidsieck & Louis Roederer. Reims has a spectacular cathedral, the size and splendour of Notre Dame.

Riddling (or Remuage) – This is a process which facilitates the settling of lees into the neck of the champagne bottle so the sediment can easily be removed by disgorgement.

Reserve Wine – Wine which is kept back in the cellar and used to blend into newer wines to achieve consistency, and add complexity and quality. Reserve wines can be aged for a long time before they are blended, in steel tank, oak barrel or in bottle. The vessel and age of the reserve wine will affect the final taste of the champagne.

Rosé – Pink champagne.

S

Sabrage – Opening champagne with a sword (sabre)! This historic method of opening bottles is dangerous and lot of fun.

Sec – Medium sweet style, which carries between 13 and 24 grams of sugar per bottle.

Secondary Fermentation – What makes champagne champagne. The secondary fermentation in bottle is what creates champagne's fizz and complex toasty flavours.

Sur Lees – Literally 'on the lees' referring to how champagne ages in contact with lees following secondary fermentation. See Lees.

Sommelier – Essentially a fancy wine waiter. Traditionally found in fine dining restaurants, now you find Somms in many different areas of the wine industry. A proper Somm will be trained in restaurants in all aspects of wine, service and cuisine, specializing in food and wine matching.

T

Terroir – No direct English translation. Terroir is the taste of 'somewhereness'. A sensory experience of place where a wine is made. It can be defined as a complex combination of nature, history, climate and geology to give a wine a unique flavour and character to where it is grown.

Tirage – The important step of adding sugar and yeast to the bottle to spark the secondary fermentation in bottle, following first fermentation.

Toast – All those lovely toasted, brioche, biscuit and creamy flavours which develop in champagne after ageing in bottle. This is due to the enzymatic breakdown of yeast cells following the second fermentation. See Autolysis.

V

Vallée de la Marne – Marne Valley is an important sub-zone of Champagne where Pinot Meunier is the dominant grape variety.

Vielles Vignes – Literally, 'Old Vines'. Older vines can give wines, and champagnes, a unique and complex style due to the small quantities of grapes old vines produce.

Vin Clair – The base clear wine of champagne, before it is blended and goes through second fermentation.

Vinification – Winemaking.

Vintage – If a vintage is written on the label, 100% of the wine must come from that year. Vintage champagne is not an indication of quality but champagne houses only produce vintage wines in good years, so you can expect a Millésime champagne to be high standard. Vintage champagnes benefit from extended ageing, if you can wait. See Millésime.

Viticulture – The science and production of grapes.

Y

Yeast – Yeast is a living, single-cell organism. When in proximity with sugar or starch it converts into alcohol and carbon dioxide.

Z

Żyw – My surname. Pronounced Zhiv! Think Dr. Zhivago.

Acknowledgements

Jenny Brown, my inspirational mum who I need to thank for so much more than being an incredible agent, who taught me to raise my horizons above the Pentland Hills. This book is dedicated to my granny **Pauline Brown** who has been and forever will be a constant source of guidance. **Yvie**, my long suffering girlfriend who deserves all the champagne in this book for her patience – I did my best to test it!

Freight for believing in this project

Françoise Peretti & **Alisa Cargill** at CIVC for their help in my research, their very generous hospitality and their courageous commitment to champagne

Richard Geoffroy at Dom Perignon for his generous time and invaluable insight, not to mention that 1973

Jean-Hervé Chiquet at Jacquesson for the rosé, that slap-up lunch and the poster

Delphine Cazals at Champagne Cazals, and her Mum! I've never flambéed prawns with Grand Cru Blanc de Blancs before

Chloé Verrat at Champagne Deutz, your tour was priceless

Ryan Apicella at Moët Hennessy UK

Stephen Leroux, **Tori Ellis** & **Willem Pinçon** at Charles Heidsieck

Kevin Wallis at Bollinger

Brigitte Hennessy & **Nicole Strozzi** at Laurent Perrier

Jean-Baptiste Lecaillon at Louis Roederer

Mark Bingley at MMD UK

Guy Nightingale at Gosset

David Galetti at Le Gavroche

Ed Nash at Lanson UK

Christian Holthausen at AR Lenoble

Ferdinand Pougatch at Champagne Virginie T

Gilles Marguet at Union de Champagne

Anselme Selosse at Selosse

John Atkinson MW at Billecart Salmon

Cassidy Dart & **Freya Miller** at Pol Roger

Vicky Major at Major PR

Leonora Findlater at Pernod Ricard

Dear thanks to **Laura Jewell**, for a lot more than just proof reading

Anna Bell at Corney & Barrow

Christophe Constant at J.L Vergnon

Joe & **Judy Hancock**

Bob McDevitt

Direct Wines

My stepdad, **Sandy Richardson**

My brothers; **Felix, Sorley, Tommy,** & **Danny**

My dad, **Adam Zyw**

Also special thanks to **Team GB,** WW!

Photography credits

Unless listed below, all photography by Freight & Davy Zyw

pg. 48 – 'Depart' by Benoit Tarlant
pg. 50 – 'André Clouet 2002' by Marcus Hansson
pg. 64 – 'Végétal' by Benoit Tarlant
pg. 92 – 'Moët & Chandon vineyards' by Joe deSousa
pg. 100 – 'Young vines in Épernay' by Pug Girl
pg. 114 – 'Clos du Mesnil vineyard' by Tomas e
pg. 116 – 'Reims Cathedral' by Daxis
pg. 146 – 'G. H. Mumm cellars' by Anna & Michal
pg. 157 – 'Château de Boursault' by Benoit Tarlant
pg. 160 – 'Caves Pommery' by Sébastien Bertrand
pg. 174 – 'Vineyards in Marne' by Luc Coekaerts
pg. 178 – 'Veuve Clicquot vineyard' by Joe deSousa